Martin Crimp's Power Plays

This book covers playwright Martin Crimp's recent work showing how it captures the nuances in our interpersonal contemporary experience.

Examining the bold and exciting body of writing by Crimp, the book delves into his depiction of intersections between narratives, as well as between private and public, through an honest look at power structures and shifts, marriages and relationships, sexuality, and desire.

This book will be of great interest to students and scholars in Drama, Theatre and Performance, English Literature, and Opera Studies.

Vicky Angelaki is Professor in English Literature at Mid Sweden University.

T0347966

Routledge Advances in Theatre & Performance Studies

This series is our home for cutting-edge, upper-level scholarly studies and edited collections. Considering theatre and performance alongside topics such as religion, politics, gender, race, ecology, and the avant-garde, titles are characterized by dynamic interventions into established subjects and innovative studies on emerging topics.

Rapa Nui Theatre
Staging Indigenous Identities in Easter Island
Moira S. Fortin Cornejo

Appropriations of Irish Drama in Modern Korean Nationalist Theatre
Hunam Yun

Martin Crimp's Power Plays
Intertextuality, Sexuality, Desire
Vicky Angelaki

Playwriting in Europe
Mapping Ecosystems and Practices with Fabulamundi
Margherita Laera

"Don't Forget The Pierrots!"
The Complete History of British Pierrot Troupes & Concert Parties
Tony Lidington

For more information about this series, please visit: https://www.routledge.com/Routledge-Advances-in-Theatre–Performance-Studies/book-series/RATPS

Martin Crimp's Power Plays

Intertextuality, Sexuality, Desire

Authored by Vicky Angelaki

Routledge
Taylor & Francis Group

LONDON AND NEW YORK

First published 2023
by Routledge
4 Park Square, Milton Park, Abingdon, Oxon OX14 4RN

and by Routledge
605 Third Avenue, New York, NY 10158

*Routledge is an imprint of the Taylor & Francis Group,
an informa business*

© 2023 Vicky Angelaki

British Library Cataloguing-in-Publication Data
A catalogue record for this book is available from the British Library

Library of Congress Cataloging-in-Publication Data
Names: Angelaki, Vicky, 1980- author.
Title: Martin Crimp's power plays : intertextuality, sexuality, desire /
authored by Vicky Angelaki.
Description: Abingdon, Oxon ; New York, NY : Routledge, 2023. |
Includes bibliographical references and index. |
Identifiers: LCCN 2022014922 (print) | LCCN 2022014923 (ebook) |
ISBN 9780367471026 (hardback) | ISBN 9781032344331 (paperback) |
ISBN 9781003033400 (ebook)
Subjects: LCSH: Crimp, Martin, 1956---Criticism and interpretation. |
English drama--21st century--History and criticism. | Interpersonal
relations in literature. | Marriage in literature. | Sex in literature. |
LCGFT: Literary criticism.
Classification: LCC PR6053.R495 Z549 2023 (print) |
LCC PR6053.R495 (ebook) | DDC 822/.914--dc23/eng/20220520
LC record available at https://lccn.loc.gov/2022014922
LC ebook record available at https://lccn.loc.gov/2022014923

ISBN: 9780367471026 (hbk)
ISBN: 9781032344331 (pbk)
ISBN: 9781003033400 (ebk)

DOI: 10.4324/9781003033400

Typeset in Bembo
by KnowledgeWorks Global Ltd.

For my dear parents, Niko and Vaso, and their
wonderful partners, Deirdre and George –
all my love, all my gratitude.

Contents

Acknowledgements

I first started researching Martin Crimp's theatre a dizzying twenty years ago – here we are, still, because Martin's work is always electric, never predictable; for that, I am as excited as I am grateful. My gratitude very much extends to Martin for kindly answering questions, facilitating resources and being supportive in a most meaningful way.

My thanks, always, to my dear colleagues and mentors: Élisabeth Angel-Perez, Chris Megson, Dan Rebellato, Elizabeth Sakellaridou, Liz Tomlin – for all our conversations and their boundless ability to motivate and inspire through the years. My warm thanks, also, to all colleagues who have offered feedback on my work on Martin Crimp through the decades, in one form or another, and who have invited me to contribute to their own volumes, events, and initiatives.

I would very much like to thank the exemplary team at Routledge, Laura Hussey and Swati Hindwan, for always being utterly available, supportive and generous – a delight to work with. My warmest thanks, also, to the anonymous peer reviewer of the proposal that became this book, for their insightful understanding. Regarding this volume, every effort has been made to ensure that quotations fall within fair dealing principles for academic publications.

On the personal front, my sincere thanks to Gull-Britt and Roberto, for their warmth and kindness. My greatest thanks, and all my love, as always, to my wonderful family: Niko, Vaso, George, Deirdre, Akis, and Pavlina. And to Stefano, my thanks, and my heart.

Vicky Angelaki, 2022

Introduction

Surveying the Battleground: Martin Crimp's Relationscapes

In one of its most shattering moments, after her recent marriage has – perhaps irreparably – disintegrated, Katrina, one half of the couple in Martin Crimp's two-hander *Play House* (2012), confronts her husband – Simon – with this speech:

> — Because you don't love me. Because you have never loved me. I've given you my whole body and all of my attention for months and months and months – and it's still not enough for you. I've given you my hopefulness and all of my wit and charm, my tolerance and a large part of my pitiful income – and it's still not enough. […] And all of that time – while I was giving you everything – you've been chipping and chipping away at my soul […].
>
> (2012a: 28)[1]

The very title of the play carries a meta-element: marriage as performance, spousal co-habitation as a form of play in and of itself. A construct, of sorts, consisting of two willing players and a certain artificiality built on a tacit, implicit, and complicit understanding of what the marriage mechanism requires to keep on running. Until, that is, events transpire that are so catastrophic and beyond redemption that the couple come to the point of confronting the profound lack, or *unplayability*, at the heart of their union. For Katrina and Simon, though in distinctive Crimp style this is never specified, it is likely that the event is Simon's suggestion to have a drug-fuelled sexual encounter with a neighbour. That the person in question works in financial services is a helpful nod to the fact that the economy, as corrosive force, can be held responsible for the disintegration of dignity and the domestic alike. As Katrina remarks, accepting the proposition as response to Simon's passive/aggressive strategy for eliciting consent, it 'feel[s] like swallowing acid' (2012a: 28).

DOI: 10.4324/9781003033400-1

For a play as short as this one is, developing in thirteen brief episodic scenes that depict a marriage between two young people from the beginning through to what we might quite plausibly imagine to be its ending, *Play House* manages to capture the devotion, desire, strife, and violence that make up a relationscape in Crimp's theatre with extraordinary coverage and precision at the same time. The violence is sometimes self-directed; sometimes directed at that matrimonial Other, especially through speech; sometimes sexual. In any case, it is always present as a force that is equally centripetal and centrifugal: if we imagine the couple as the core, or nucleus, then it is the outside world – especially one where financial survival, or power of authority are at stake – that equally determines and is determined by the forces of tension at large in that household, in Crimp's unhospitable domestic warzones. First staged with the older text *Definitely the Bahamas* (1987) as a double bill at the Orange Tree Theatre, Richmond, where Crimp's career as a playwright began in the early 1980s, *Play House* offered the opportunity for an up-to-date pulse-taking on where Crimp's theatre stood on marriage but also, at the same time, for the exposition of how patterns of domestic politics, acceptance, and violence – mental, emotional, physical, and actual or threatened – are passed down from one generation to the next. It was quite meaningful that the production landed in 2012, thirty years after Crimp's first ever play to be performed at the Orange Tree Theatre, *Living Remains* (1982). The primary event of *Definitely the Bahamas*, an otherwise quiet and subdued play, is one older couple's voluntary blindness to and covering up of the fact that their son has been sexually transgressive against at least one woman while, at the same time, keeping up the pretences of his own marriage. With a writer as active as Crimp we cannot talk about coming full circle, but we can, perhaps, talk about stock-taking, or checking-in moments that connect one's past, present, and future as an artist. Given the meaningfulness of the Orange Tree Theatre to Crimp's overall artistic narrative, as well as the fact that Crimp himself directed this double bill, this was one such moment.

In the realm of Crimp's writing, irrespective of genre, the concept of a content romantic relationship and/or marriage is untenable. The habitat of a relationship, that space that develops between any two people intimately connected to each other, is never safe. The ecology is always perturbed both from outside and within. It is a streak of conflict and turmoil that is electrified not only by external conditions and their essential and undeniable impact on the private, but also from the characters' own desire for undoing – because in Crimp's work desire is, of course, sexual, but it is also an urge and a profound need to test the self to the limit, even if that act forges a path towards one's own undoing. It is this defiant – and also self-defiant – act, against any instinct of preservation, because the desire is stronger, that is primal, however much it may be filtered through the sophisticated gaze and analyses of Crimp's characters that we witness, especially in Crimp's most recent work. It is that same act that leads Jocasta and Laios, with the fiery trail of whose sex life Crimp is concerned in *The Rest Will Be Familiar to You from Cinema* (2013) picking up from Euripides, to have the carnal relationship that will produce a child, even knowing, as per the oracle, that this son is destined to commit the ultimate act of violence against his father and displace him as his mother's partner. Pushing to the limits, as this later work by Crimp shows, comes with its own allure: physical, emotional, even mental – that renders transgression not merely inevitable, since Crimp's characters are not fatalists, but, actually, appealing, and a choice – because Crimp's characters are fascinated by the prospect and execution of such precarious exercises.

As the texts that this book is concerned with show us, the consequences of pursuing these acts of desire extend beyond the private and into the public. *Lessons in Love and Violence* (2018) emphatically proves this point, for example, as a King surrenders to longing so completely that his own political narrative becomes obliterated. These acts, are, then, pursued methodically and with conviction, as *When We Have Sufficiently Tortured Each Other* (2019) also poignantly goes on to demonstrate: an exercise in boundary stretching so absolute, that any constant is thrown into utter disarray. The outcome may be, much of the time, catastrophic. It is so in Crimp's reworking of *Cyrano de Bergerac* (2019), which follows not only the titular character's desire, but also the desire of the one he is fully surrendered to as his only compass, painfully aware of the outcome of such a path, yet, equally, defiant. It is this sense of knowingly disrupting one's ease, and purposefully injecting disequilibrium, against settling, or against the writing of a smooth and expected finale to one's own story – which is studied with the precision that someone else's story might have been studied with – that also drives the endeavour in work such as *Men Asleep* (2018).

But what brought us here? As I am writing this Introduction, Crimp's writing for the theatre spans over four decades. During this time, marriage and relationships have featured prominently in his work – and although it is fair to say that they have always been laden with a certain amount of conflict, the grounds for this conflict have never been simple, or straightforward. A reason for this is that it tends to be linked to the writing – but even more often the re-writing – of personal history. The fact that Crimp has often worked intertextually provides this process with an additional layer of complexity. The inner threads become infinitely more tangled when the private domain is part of the public, not only in the symbiotic sense of society operating in tandem with the individual and vice versa, but also because the protagonists of the plays are quite explicitly public figures. Truth is always at stake in the relationships that Crimp's theatre delves into, from the personal truth of how one views themselves in a relationship/partnership/ marriage to how they view the other person – and indeed how they are viewed by them. The kaleidoscopic image of the domestic plays and the fact that there is no such thing as one simple truth, as well as that any interpersonal circumstance has facets that will remain necessarily hidden, because the extent of our knowledge of the other person can only take us that far, is a constant. When Crimp's characters step outside of the playing rules of their domestic arrangements – seeking, if not complete truth, then, at least, a greater sense of clarity – because they are compelled, instinctively, almost, to do so, rather than because it is strategically sound, revelations land torrentially and the landscape changes dramatically and irretrievably. Different couples in Crimp's theatre handle this aftermath in different ways: for some the relationship is suspended; for others it continues on a new, complicit understanding; for others, the chances of any co-existence are irretrievably destroyed. But what does not change, despite these multifaceted and nuanced conflicts, is the power tug of war. Again, it is helpful to remember that, in some cases, this does not only denote power on the domestic level, but also actual political, or state power.

To better understand the evolution in Crimp's theatre and the way in which intertextuality has afforded him a deepening of his engagement with issues relating to power play on an expanded sphere clearly crossing over into the political by way of history, including, of course, the history of the literary and artistic canon, it serves us to consider a selected overview. Given the thematic context of this book, which is concerned with the post-2013 period, in order to ground the ensuing discussion and produce a sense of continuity, it is necessary here to consider, briefly, what precedes the main focal area of the present publication.[2] Additionally, it is purposeful to clarify that the reason for which this publication is concerned with the specific time period is twofold: firstly, this is because I have covered the earlier years in Crimp's career extensively in a number of previous publications, and, especially, my books *The Plays of Martin Crimp: Making Theatre Strange* (2012) and *Social and Political Theatre in Twenty-First-Century Britain: Staging Crisis* (2017); secondly, it is because the intertextual element, and the historical engagement with canons literary and artistic through the exploration of diachronically urgent concerns refracted via Crimp's most distinctive angle of vision produces a rich, diverse, and, yet, interconnected narrative that can be accounted for within the remit of one such cohesive analysis.

The format of the Advances series allows me the ideal framework for such a discussion: a decade is precisely the amount of space and time that a publication of this scope and length can claim to cover in a meaningful way. As with any discussion of the contemporary, this, too, does not claim to be exhaustive, nor is that its primary intention; this is a shorter-length monograph that is aware of its own stipulations and limitations in terms of terrain. Each chapter ends with 'Closing Reflections', rather than a 'Conclusion' as such. Similarly, the final section is entitled 'Afterword' rather than 'Conclusion'. Such choices are indicative of the fact that it is not my intention to proclaim my discoveries final, or my conclusions absolute. This would not be of service to the nature of the texts themselves. It is my intention, however, as an academic author with a consistent engagement with Crimp's challenging, complex, layered work over a two-decade period, to trace what it is that so resolutely, yet, also, so delicately, serves to interconnect these plays. As I contend in my title, intertextuality, sexuality, and desire, which this book will alternate in highlighting in the ensuing discussion, serve as primary and essential grounding factors for the plays and for my analysis equally.

In the ensuing chapters, the book consistently prioritizes Crimp's texts rather than embark upon analyses of the source material from which we might say it stems, or with which it is in dialogue. As I have also discussed in my earlier monograph on Crimp, in cases of new texts such as *Cruel and Tender*, and such as the work that I am dealing with here, Crimp's artistic agency is so heightened that we are dealing with pieces that carry their own weight and significance. In other words: these are not strictly versions, or updatings; they are radical departures. As such, they both merit and claim the emphasis, and the purpose of this book is not to compare and/or contrast. In some cases, decisions have been made as to the pairing of texts, in the hope that their cross-consideration might enhance their individual understanding in the context of establishing broader sensibilities. Likewise, it will be helpful to the reader to note that this monograph, once more, aware of its length and spatial limitations, remains focused on its priority: the recent work of Martin Crimp through the lens of specific thematic concerns, focusing on intertextuality, sexuality and desire as angles that, given the form and content of this book, are identified as of primary relevance for a coherent and cohesive discussion. The aim of this book, however, is not to provide an exhaustive theorization of the terms, on which ample critical and theoretical discourse is, in any case, already available. Such cannot be the purview of this monograph, which concentrates on a playwright's work and the texts themselves as the primary point of departure. Following a consideration of the artistic history that brings us to the present time, then, this Introduction will proceed with an elaboration as to the overall approach and interpretative journey of this book.

Tentative Textures of Intimacy: Looking Back on Crimp's Complex Couples

Further to *Definitely the Bahamas*, the other standout Crimp text of the 1980s in the context of marriage and relationships is *Dealing with Clair* (1988), whose enduring resonance was underlined when it was revived by the same theatre that first commissioned it, once more Richmond's Orange Tree Theatre, in 2018, directed by Richard Twyman. The couple at the centre of the play, Liz and Mike, are married, young parents and upwardly mobile. This is, in fact, one of the 'healthier' marriages that we encounter in Crimp's playwriting; the couple stay together; there is no major conflict. Still, that does not mean that there are no undercurrents – on the contrary. Part of Liz and Mike's bond rests on their implicit understanding, very much connected to the original social context of the play, Thatcher's neoliberalism, in terms of the deification of property ownership and individual progress. The couple's commitment to each other derives from and rests on their likewise shared commitment to material advancement. This is, also, what gives rise to the action in the play: the sale of the couple's house mobilizes an entire web of deceit and violence that will eventually lead to the disappearance of the young female estate agent who is handling the sale – the guilty party, though never clearly stated, is, by all obvious accounts, the man who has been posing as a legitimate buyer and who is, in fact, a sociopathic criminal. But the deceit begins from the couple's attachment to their profit plan, which includes maximizing the sale potential of a house that has flaws, from permanent stains on the carpet to a windowless room that is presented as a guest bedroom. There is also a degree of tension – albeit subtle – in Liz and Mike's relationship: their au-pair, Anna, is a reminder of the sexuality that has perhaps been somewhat compromised by recent motherhood for Liz and, despite the humorous tone of these exchanges, the references to Anna's appearance reveal a sexual appetite from Mike and its tacit recognition by Liz. This will go on to become somewhat more disturbing later, when, in a late-night conversation, Liz jokingly confronts Mike as to his sexual feelings towards Clair. More than an accusation, the acknowledgement appears to empower Liz, who prefers to show that she knows rather than pretend not to see. In terms of exposing predatorial systemic attitudes against women, the play is, of course, ahead of the curve. Ultimately, when we assess this couple, what emerges as the balancing element in their relationship is the fact that transgressive thoughts are allowed, as long as they are not acted upon. This is a very carefully choreographed co-existence, where the balance of power stays precisely so, in order for Liz and Mike's neoliberalist life to continue in its mould, intact.

A few years later *The Treatment* (1993) would deliver one of the most stinging portrayals of marital life hinging on power, complicity, and exploitation. Here, Jennifer and Andrew, two New York film producers, equally committed to their professional and financial advancement, draw into their world the inexperienced author Anne, a woman who begins working with them towards a film version of her life's story. The metatextual element is particularly strong, with the line between Anne's actual life and the story of the film eventually crossing every possible boundary. Anne becomes a pawn in Jennifer and Andrew's power play, whereby they attempt to assert their authority over the creative process – as well as over each other – with no hesitation in setting Anne up both emotionally and artistically as part of a wider web of exploitation towards achieving their goal of a film that will be commercially successful. Soon after the film is completed, Anne fully cast aside in the creative process, she is killed by Jennifer, in an act of proclaimed accidental shooting and self-defence. In Jennifer and Andrew's no-holds-barred partnership, Anne is the sacrifice. *The Treatment* is, once more, an early nod to the importance of stage exposure of cycles of abuse, mental, emotional, and physical, in marriages, as in relationships more broadly. Anne experiences these cycles in her sexual and professional relationship with Andrew, as well as in her marriage to Simon. It is the attempt to escape the latter and forge a new path that leads Anne to the exploitative practices of Jennifer and Andrew, of which, in the beginning, she is, of course, unaware. A timely revival of the play at London's Almeida in 2017, directed by Lyndsey Turner, captured the essence of the work as speaking equally to its original cultural moment as to the contemporary one, mere months before #MeToo landed as a powerful movement towards exposition and justice for female survivors of oppression and victimization, not least in the film industry world, where the play locates its primary action.

Complicity persisted as a dominant force in Crimp's depiction of marriagescapes in *The Country* (2000). The central conflict in this play, which revolves around three characters – Corinne, Rebecca, and Richard – originates in complex deceit, perpetrated by Richard. A substantial reason why this deceit has been chronically enabled, though, concerns Corinne, his wife. Further to that of the married couple, there is another central relationship in the play: that between Rebecca and Richard. Richard is a doctor and also a drug addict; part of the allure of his affair with Rebecca has been the sharing of this addiction. In their relationship, Richard, who appears to have systematically provided Rebecca with drugs, appears – at least initially – to hold the power. Rebecca's move to the country for the purposes of her research, however, upsets the balance, propelling a move for Richard and Corinne as well. Corinne is, of course, unaware of the true grounds behind the move; Richard has presented it as an act towards salvaging the marriage, attached to a promise of sobriety. Until Rebecca is unexpectedly brought to the couple's home one night after having overdosed in Richard's car, the pretence holds. From that point onwards, however, as events unravel, so do revelations. Power negotiations are ferocious, occurring in taut dialogues that only ever involve two of the three characters at the same time. At stake are the truth and survival of a marriage, but also the survival of one's very sense of self. For Corinne to accept that Richard will be committed to the marriage going forward – as he remains both accommodating and elusive, and certainly spare with explanations – it will take a surrender of her power to him. Trust, as such, at least by the end of the play, appears impossible. On the surface, it might appear that Corinne is the powerful one – knowing, yet not revealing, the truth about Richard's addiction; forgiving; coming across as strong and magnanimous. In reality, she is as tenuous as the relationship; profoundly unhappy and uncertain. The only level of control comes from complicity, and whether this will ultimately be enough to sustain a marriage is a question whose resolution we do not get to witness before curtain call.

With 2004's *Cruel and Tender* came a spectacular opening up of Crimp's canvas owing to intertextuality and adaptation as they materialized through his bold and highly successful foray into Greek tragedy. In terms of origins, content and style, *Cruel and Tender* is the text that lies closest to the primary case studies of this book. The scale of the marriage it is concerned with is an epic one: two characters that could be summed up as – equally – forces of nature find themselves in the context of a conflict that becomes all-encompassing, leading to their respective annihilation. The female lead is Amelia: a highly intelligent woman who married the General, her until recently high-ranking military husband, at a young age and became a mother, only to become sidelined as years passed, displaced by the General's desire for war as well as a younger woman. When we encounter Amelia, this woman, Laela, has been brought into her home while the General is still missing in action. It is Amelia's unwitting exposure of the General to a corrosive chemical substance, that she mistakenly believes will cause nostalgia [in the Greek sense of the painful longing for home], sent to him via their son, that does, indeed cause him to return. He is, however, brought back by the government he was enlisted to serve under highly unceremonious circumstances, a war criminal in serious mental and physical decline, unable to control either his mind or body. It is a thoroughly plausible – on the terms of the brutality of the War on Terror, the context in which the play premiered – hypothesis, even though Crimp far from ties the action to any military conflict happening at that given point in time. Although the violence of the battlefield never pales as a reference, it is the brutality of marriage, captured in the separate stage times and presences of two profoundly emotionally saturated individuals who never meet on stage, that emerges as the dominant concern. The devastated, war-torn landscapes that the General describes are perfect metaphors for the ravaged expanses of the characters' emotional worlds. As one of Crimp's most staggering female characters, Amelia emerges as the shattering human vessel of, equally, tenderness and cruelty, depicting how both can simultaneously inhabit the same person as, beyond counterbalances, an essential synthesis of fierceness and vulnerability. The Sophoclean span of emotions finds an ideal partner in Crimp, who reaches beyond adaptation to sense the inner rhythm of the text and flesh it out into the first years of the twenty-first century, where a radical uncertainty prevails, particularly after 9/11, beginning to make itself manifest in all intersecting aspects of life, personal, social, and political.

The cruelty in marriages, often submerged under the tepid waters of everyday co-existence, makes its re-appearance in *Fewer Emergencies* (particularly the 2005 version), which begins with the line 'She gets married very young, doesn't she' (Crimp 2005a: 7), thrusting the spectator right in the mental and emotional crisis of a woman who remains unnamed, and whose life equally unnamed voices narrate, or devise, like a plot, or a script. The generic interchangeability of the faulty marriage pattern emerges strongly in a play that is in an intertextual relationship with itself, consisting of three shorter texts (*Whole Blue Sky*, *Face to the Wall* and *Fewer Emergencies*), which unfold into one another. As the play examines the gradual suppression of desire and its sacrifice to the temple of convenience, the human casualties of such fraught contexts appear no less monumental than the epic figures we encounter in Crimp's adaptations of the classics. But it is the intertextual ripple effect of the play's storyline towards itself that sets the tone for a bigger event, which would become fully manifest three years later (2008), when Crimp's *The City*, as *Die Stadt*, premiered in Berlin, followed, shortly afterwards, by a London production.

Clair, the lead figure in this play, is a translator, but also a writer. She is married to Chris, with whom she may or may not have children – one of these is a Girl, an intriguing character, whose overall unplaceability and overwhelming strangeness might suggest to the spectators that Clair's family life is far from idyllic, or even predictable. The marriage itself is problematic: the distribution of power between the two characters fluctuates, but it is, in any case, unequal. The relationship itself is contentious. When Clair and Chris talk, whether regarding their everyday, or, more specifically, as this is the centre towards which their conversations tend to gravitate, their work (including, at times, its lack), there is almost the impression that they exist in parallel discourses. There is a sense of unfamiliarity towards the person that one is, arguably, expected to be the closest to, but also a profound absence of affection between the two. Occasionally, there is also micro-aggression, evidence, in itself, of a macro-aggression that has long shaped the balance of the marriage. Career dissatisfaction on both sides is a factor; a lack of intimacy and excitement in the marriage is another. All this escalates when, in the final scene of the play, it is revealed that Chris, like everyone else in the domain of the action we have been following, is an imaginary character. Clair, that is, has been writing fiction, or at least attempting to, and the storyline of her marriage, her motherhood, even her work, are, now, all revealed as such: unreal and untenable. Inspiration is lacking; like the marriage itself, so Clair's fictional narrative lacks substance and sustenance. *The City* is significant for a number of reasons in Crimp's theatre; for the purposes of this book it speaks directly to both the theme of hidden plotlines existing between couples, complete with power shifts, and the engagement with and exposition of the complexities of storytelling, the revision of narratives, unexpected plot twists and inconclusive stories – or indeed histories, as we come to witness in subsequent work.

One of the fundamental accomplishments of *In the Republic of Happiness*, Crimp's next major work in 2012, was that it read – and felt – as though it were three distinct texts, intersecting intertextually across different forms. The first part of the play is naturalist; the second is abstract; the third is reminiscent of Crimp's unique style of what we might describe as quietly surrealist: there is a considerable degree of plausibility in the exchange between characters, yet, we know that on the basis of what we hold to be real, or mundane, the conversation cannot be taking place on any plane of experience that we broadly associate with the everyday – and so it is dreamlike, haunting, suspended. That this moment in the play revolves around a couple – Madeleine and Bob – to whom we are first introduced in the opening part of the play, is telling: on the one hand, because of the intertextual discourse that the play establishes with itself, after it has broken all narrative sequence in its middle part; on the other hand, because, once more, it is a couple that is at the heart of textual recalibration – trying to regain its core through different iterations of the union. In the beginning, we see Madeleine and Bob as part of a family scene, announcing their imminent departure and break from their relatives; a collapse of all setting and character follows in the middle part; in the end, we encounter the couple alone, in their own indeterminate sphere of being, where the marriage (not an especially happy one) is both the gravitational pole of all that exists and, at the same time, unable to sustain the characters' existence solely unto itself. The echoes of Bob's sexually transgressive past, hinted at in the first part of the play, linger; so do Madeleine's domineering instincts. Crimp presents us with a marriage that is both inevitable and impossible – an electric, short-circuiting dynamic that, without ever overlapping with itself, Crimp's theatre has explored in different versions, not least in the more recent texts, on which I concentrate in the following chapters.

The same year saw a significant event in the realm of Crimp's cross-genre writing: the George Benjamin opera *Written on Skin*, for which Crimp wrote the text proceeding from a pre-existing folk narrative, and which I have previously discussed in detail elsewhere. When a man – The Protector – commissions the creation of an illuminated manuscript, the artist who undertakes the task becomes his wife's object of desire; but he also awakens desire in The Protector himself, in what continues Crimp's foray into sexuality beyond heterosexual norms, a concern that he had also explored in his version of Ferdinand Bruckner's *Pains of Youth* (2009). There, two women found themselves entangled in a play of power and lust that would only become resolved by death, as a way of escaping the banality of bourgeoisie, looming as an otherwise inexorable force suppressing individual urges. The layers of intertextuality at play in *Written on Skin* are remarkable, from the primary level of Crimp's engagement with a found story, to the fact that the opera follows the creation of a new narrative – the illuminated book. This will come to tell the story of the household itself, including the affair. And then, there are the figures that, in the production, serve as curators in the present, existing on a supra-level above the story: they are the 'angels', figures extrinsic to the main plot itself, who engage in the cataloguing of the archaeologies of desire, archiving and filing it, as shown in Vicki Mortimer's set of two levels – one for the action of the past, one for that of the present, towards the future. While the artist – or The Boy – is the catalyst for the escalation of events, it is the fraught exchange of power between The Protector and Agnès, his wife, that serves as the centre of the piece. It is a gender battle, but also a battle of wills – and desires, where the one who has assumed power for himself is quietly usurped by the one who asserts her right to choice – and to freedom, first in life, through the affair, and then in death, through her suicide. The Boy's body in life and in death is the ground on which the battle of desires comes to play out – but it is the individual, distinct poles of the married couple that are set up as the primary plot bearers. Their conflict is as primal as it is mundane, as diachronic as it is urgent. The stakes are both petty and familiar (perseverance and the emergence of the stronger partner), just as they are also grandiose and vast: a matter of actual survival with long-stretching consequences. These concern the tales and paradigms of marriage that we inherit, and, in turn, their impact on our understanding of how relational and relative the gravities of the domestic are for wider public models of gender domination and socio-political consequence, especially where privilege translates as power.

The work that follows *Written on Skin* expands upon the hypothesis, opening up to an array of different directions. As this book will discuss, drawing on the recent publication of Crimp's collection *Writing for Nothing* (2019), which presents a range of texts in the opera, short fiction and short play genres, there is a strong sense of the meta-theatrical and meta-representational more broadly emanating across the board, including these shorter pieces. Drawing on this collection, the first chapter of this book, 'Imitating Art: Fiction Pieces and Short Plays' will examine how texts like 'The Play' and *The Art of Painting*, emblematic for their significance in this group of texts and aligned with the concerns of the present discussion, perform their own entanglement in intricate artistic narratives. Specifically, the chapter will explore how this is shaped in the context of storylines unfolding within the theatre industry ('The Play'), or of art as trigger and stimulant, both embedding and becoming embedded in the beholder (*The Art of Painting*), who superscribes their own narrative on the object. I will further probe how such texts suggest that there is always a by-default performativity in social constructs – and a certain pleasure in recognizing this, whether through literary framing, or through self-staging and the resulting mediation as a form of spectacle.

The next chapter, 'Mating for Life: *Men Asleep*', concentrates on how the specific play (2018) continues Crimp's intertextual journey, while delivering a new piece of theatre that develops a dialogue with two pre-existing texts, though only one of them is literary. Specifically, Crimp draws on Edward Albee's play *Who's Afraid of Virginia Woolf* (1962), as well as Maria Lassnig's painting *Schlafende Männer* [*Men Asleep*] (2006), which also lends Crimp's play its title. We are firmly in the present here: action is located in the urban apartment of a middle-aged, middle-class couple, Julia and Paul. Over the course of one night their lives will become transformed in Crimp's characteristic mode of subtext and implication rather than revelation and disclosure. Late into the night, Julia and Paul receive a visit by the younger couple of Josefine and Tilman. As the couples become acquainted, so the finer details of their marriages and the base on which they are respectively constituted begin to emerge. Generational gaps and differing approaches to work-life balance and ideologies regarding having children, or not, make for fissures, not only inter- but also intra-couple, revealing profound anxieties, senses of lack and repressed desires. The field is rendered more complex still by an additional tension factor. Whereas the women emerge as impressive workers (both academics), the men (one academic/artist and one entrepreneur), however successful, lack sharp focus and ambition. But if the bond that develops between the women can be thought of as an offshoot of the maternal – with all the complexities this might entail – the bond that emerges between the men is erotic. After all, in Lassnig's painting women are conspicuously absent and the play develops a through-line to this narrative. But a particularly important element, further to the power politics developing between the four characters, concerns the differing approaches to marriage: from the – seemingly – resolutely childless couple (Julia and Paul) with a reduced sex drive to the couple (Josefine and Tilman) in the early stages of pregnancy, with an active sexual desire for one another, Crimp's play explores what it means to mate for life, and how that very life may, in fact, prove most fragile.

With sexuality as enactment emerging not only as strong concern but, rather, as plot pivot in this recent body of work by Crimp, two texts capture this theme especially emphatically: *Cyrano de Bergerac* and *When We Have Sufficiently Tortured Each Other* (both 2019). With the chapter 'Handling with Care: *Cyrano de Bergerac* and *When We Have Sufficiently Tortured Each Other*', the foray into intertextuality continues, this time in dialogue with, in the first case, Edmond Rostand's eponymous piece (1897) and, in the second, Samuel Richardson's *Pamela; or, Virtue Rewarded* (1740; the subtitle of Crimp's play is *Twelve Variations on*

Samuel Richardson's Pamela). Reminiscent of earlier work by Crimp and especially *Attempts on Her Life*, but also of the recent texts that this book concentrates on, this play develops in episodes, or vignettes. Unlike *Attempts on Her Life*, however, these might be described as sequential, registering a response to events as we observe them in the Richardson text, which, other than this cross-reference, Crimp's play does not emulate in aesthetics, shifting its action to the contemporary moment, as is the case with *Cyrano*. Even though the dramaturgical approach to the opening production at the National Theatre (London) directed by Katie Mitchell did not necessarily reflect the structure of Crimp's text, favouring, rather, a continuous flow of action, Crimp's play is also in dialogue with *The City*, given that in both a couple's life is usurped by a string of guest characters, whether seen or unseen, and, equally importantly, objects, which are unexpectedly integrated into the plot, emphasizing the artificiality of the domestic as construct and social convention. Whereas in *The City* it is the economy that emerges as the primary corrosive element, here the antagonist to marriage that threatens to throw it into disequilibrium is the confinement experienced within institutional structures and the systemic categorization of female and male stereotypes, the (de)legitimization of desire, and the dominance of one gender's desire over another's. Suitably, part of Crimp's critique of long-entrenched heteronormative structures is, also, to throw gender binarism into rightful disarray. Marriage, in this play, appears almost incidental; this is mostly a text that is invested in exposing the concentration and distribution of power: across society, but also, as an essential consequence of the social, embodied experience between partners in a sexual relationship. Arguably Crimp's boldest and most sexually charged play to date – a reference I make with relevance to the text rather than the considerable liberty taken in the production, which rendered this sexuality explicit – *When We Have Sufficiently Tortured Each Other* is a play for our time: for sexual and gender fluidity, for #MeToo and #TimesUp, for asking on what terms an equal partnership – and the equal access to pleasure – might come to be constituted.

The concerns persist in *Cyrano de Bergerac*. A woman's desire sets the plot of the play in motion, when Roxane seeks solace in her confidant, Cyrano, regarding how she might progress the sequence of events that will surrender to her the object of her desire: the handsome soldier Christian. Roxane emerges as an ideal, as intellectually formidable as she is beautiful, an almost impossible match for any partner. So her match can only be embodied by two, as one person alone cannot suffice: Christian, who embodies the physical attraction, and Cyrano, who serves as the intellectual allure, lending his words to Christian, who performs Cyrano, as much as Cyrano performs Christian. But much as the process is built on the premise of being seamless, this cannot come to pass; boundaries evaporate and fluidities emerge, not only in terms of how Roxane perceives the two men, but, also, in terms of how they come to perceive each other. The aesthetics of Jamie Lloyd's production, polished, modern, and resisting the antiquated urge to use prosthetics for the stage representation of Cyrano's considerable nose, blurred boundaries further. As this chapter goes on to address, fluidities of appearance, gender, sexuality, and desire served not only to update the narrative, but, more importantly, to deliver a performance that was highly responsive to the ways in which individuals and societies have been increasingly redefining themselves, moving away from extant binary dichotomies.

The book continues and closes its main analysis with the final chapter, 'Falling Tragically: *The Rest Will Be Familiar to You from Cinema* and *Lessons in Love and Violence*'. *The Rest Will Be Familiar to You from Cinema*, opening as *Alles Weitere kennen Sie aus dem Kino* at the Deutsches Schauspielhaus Hamburg in 2013, was directed by Katie Mitchell and first published in English in 2019 as part of *The Hamburg Plays* (the other being *Men Asleep*). This play opens up to concerns surrounding the mythology of marriage, with the central union, that between Jocasta and Oedipus, serving as a vessel and source of secrets and grief, a parable for human agency versus fatalism in the face of history. The play examines the fall of the house of the Labdacides (or Labdakides) and the structure of the play is such that here, too, we observe the performativity in the archetypal roles embedded within families: wife, husband, mother, father, sister, brother – and why they are so precarious in the face of historical responsibility. Crimp returns to a concern he previously explored in *Cruel and Tender*, pursuing the problematic and by-default non-binary entanglements between personal and political, asking how individual transgressions stand to shape the course not only of one's own, but also of collective histories. As such, marriage, fuelled by desire and ambition, becomes the ultimate locus of transgression, delivering the most destructive of developments. But beyond the story at its core, the legacies of the doomed union and the genealogies of catastrophe, Crimp's text stands out also because, in the context of marriage and family, it goes a considerable way towards subverting gender stereotypes, as well as the social and political constructs that accompany them. These include the unfair expectations and limitations society and institutional structures impose on women, which, as the play invites us to consider, ought to be decisively dismantled. As this chapter will propose, Crimp's intertextual handling of his characters preserves them from emerging as irrelevant relics of the past, energizing them through imbuing resonance in the fact that their humanity is as much visible in their desire as it is in their failure.

The chapter, additionally, looks at *Lessons in Love and Violence* (2018), the latest in a series of successful collaborations with Benjamin, where Crimp returns to the topic of public marriages through intertextual exploration, delivering yet another strong text for contemporary opera. The historical field here is the reign of King Edward II, although in Crimp's work the action is thoroughly modernized and the character is only known as 'King'. As in the historical source material, the King's favouritism towards his trusted advisor, Gaveston, leads to personal and political turmoil to a ravaging extent. The crisis in the King's marriage becomes a political and historical event, escalating developments that have major repercussions for lives affected well beyond the four walls of the palace. So even though we encounter Crimp's domestic themes, the historical chronicle moves one step further than even *The Rest Will Be Familiar to You from Cinema*: in contrast with the domestic and political ruins of that play, here we come to experience the very process of ruination as outcome of desire, but while the personal downfall appears inevitable, the political stakes appear to still allow space for intervention, which is, however, not taken up. Moreover, Crimp delivers a further note of significance here: a subversion of the hegemonic, heteronormative, institutional narratives of government, love, and propriety. The fluidity in the King's sexuality as captured in the depiction of his relationship with Gaveston is crushed between public duty and marriage. The lyricism with which Crimp captures the pathos marks a substantial departure from his previous forays into relationships as a battleground where characters collide on the basis of secrets, financial failure or shifting expectations. Here, an additional factor is introduced: the clash with the familiar because of a change within the subject that is emotional as much as libidinal – a departure from one's formerly sanctioned self.

The book, as has been detailed, works on three key terms: intertextuality, sexuality, and desire. I consider these interconnected in the domain of the texts that this book is concerned with. The intertextual forays offer particularly fertile ground, through a diachronic engagement of human nature cross-genre, for establishing how it is that sexualities evolve and desires determine the ripples of history and humanity. There is considerable complexity in Crimp's intertextuality: if all lives are narratives, and each character is a text to be written, read and modified on the basis of the beholder's preferences and urges, then we operate well beyond the level of assessing the intertextual provenance of the texts examined here. It is important to remember the epistolary element in some of this work, or the active self-narration as devices: these, alongside the super- and para-texts of history that Crimp is also concerned with here, offer rich layers of meaning. Characters are forever blended storylines, facing themselves as much as their embeddedness in a fleshy narrative of society and/or politics. They are by-default intertextual in the ways their own narratives cross wires. The *Oxford English Dictionary* defines intertextuality as 'The need for one text to be read in the light of its allusions to and differences from the content or structure of other texts; the (allusive) relationship between esp. literary texts' (*Oxford English Dictionary* 2021b). It is important, here, to note the 'need': towards an understanding; because texts require a recognition as intermeshed, kneaded bodies of matter in a mélange of allusion and interdependence, much as the characters themselves.

Sexuality, of course, is also a text, or narrative: one to be cross-read, cross-examined, revisited, and revised. The *OED* defines it as, selectively, 'Sexual nature, instinct, or feelings; the possession or expression of these'; 'A person's sexual identity in relation to the gender to which he or she is typically attracted; the fact of being heterosexual, homosexual, or bisexual; sexual orientation' (*Oxford English Dictionary* 2021c). This book, likewise, approaches sexuality as both inwardly experienced and outwardly directed, but it also disposes of the 'or' when it comes to sexual orientation, following the sensibility of these texts that do not appear interested in establishing rigid lines. The book is also concerned with tracing how Crimp undermines the assumption as to how an individual might become 'typically attracted', and to whom.

Without in any way arguing that intertextuality and sexuality are simple terms, when we attempt to define desire, it proves to be yet more elusive. In the *OED*, it could be 'The fact or condition of desiring; that feeling or emotion which is directed to the attainment or possession of some object from which pleasure or satisfaction is expected; longing, craving; a particular instance of this feeling, a wish' or 'Physical or sensual appetite; lust', or indeed, also, 'A wish as expressed or stated in words; a request, petition' (*Oxford English Dictionary* 2021a). Desire, then, captures the full range of wanting, from emotion, to reason, to flesh; from love, to sex, to impetus, to rationale, and I hope, in turn, to illuminate these concerns in the following pages.

For now, however, it feels fitting to close this Introduction by persisting on desire as dominant. In a critical survey of the ways in which sexuality is verbalized, enters discourse, becomes socially conditioned, experiences fluctuations, and emerges as a key determiner of human existence, interdisciplinary sociologist Jeffrey Weeks notes the following:

> Desire is a term that lies at the heart of sexuality. It suggests a longing for the other that demands satisfaction, and perhaps can never fully be satisfied. It unsettles, destabilizes, overwhelms, dominates, is willful, playful, pleasurable, painful and always falls short of fulfilment. It is constantly repressed, […] but is seemingly irrepressible.
>
> (2011: 39)

As the book addresses such concerns in the chapters that follow, it aims to account for Martin Crimp's recent work, which, as unpredictable as ever, continues to engage with desire, sexuality, power, and politics in novel ways, delivering the kind of versatility and resistance to inflexible definitions and analyses that have long defined Crimp's writing. By considering how, in the recent period, Crimp's international collaborations have become even more extensive, with high-profile commissions and the further expansion of his industry impact, this book will also consider how, during this time, Crimp has once more reimagined the field of his writing, engaging in a series of bold intertextual exercises, whose episodic, language-driven, dialectical experimentation format moves into new artistic territory, stretching the boundaries of adaptation. Even though we might say that relationships, marriage, gender, and sexuality always alongside the impact of the personal on the political, or, more broadly, the social, are familiar territory for Crimp, what is different in this constellation of texts is a further evolution in the author's language; a newly charged boldness and sharpness of speech vis-à-vis an increasingly more difficult to define and control domain of public life, including its systemic structures, which, as these texts render evident, invite urgent reconsideration.

Notes

1. Throughout the book, where dates are indicated following the citation of a play's title, or of a text of any nature, they refer to date of premiere and/or first publication; this may mean a discrepancy between such a date and the date provided in the respective bibliographical note, which always refers to the date and context of the publication I have engaged with for the purposes of this book.
2. Given my previous work on Crimp's theatre, this section, which also covers texts I have written about in previous publications and especially in my book *The Plays of Martin Crimp: Making Theatre Strange* (2012), does not aim to be exhaustive but, rather, to touch upon the texts most directly relevant to the present discourse.

Bibliography

Angelaki, V. (2012) *The Plays of Martin Crimp: Making Theatre Strange*. Basingstoke: Palgrave Macmillan.

Angelaki, V. (2017) *Social and Political Theatre in Twenty-First-Century Britain: Staging Crisis*. London: Bloomsbury.

Crimp, M. (1982) *Living Remains*. Unpublished.

Crimp, M. (1993) *The Treatment*. London: Faber & Faber.

Crimp, M. (1997) *Attempts on Her Life*. London: Faber & Faber.

Crimp, M. (2000a) *The Country*. London: Faber & Faber.

Crimp, M. (2004) *Cruel and Tender*. London: Faber & Faber.

Crimp, M. (2005a) *Fewer Emergencies*. London: Faber & Faber.

Crimp, M. (2008) *The City*. London: Faber & Faber.

Crimp, M. (2012a) *Play House and Definitely the Bahamas*. London: Faber & Faber.

Crimp, M. (2012b) *In the Republic of Happiness*. London: Faber & Faber.

Crimp, M. (2018a) *Dealing with Clair*. London: Nick Hern Books.

Crimp, M. (2019a) *The Art of Painting*, in Crimp, M. *Writing for Nothing*. London: Faber & Faber, pp. 107–113.

Crimp, M. (2019b) *Cyrano de Bergerac – Freely Adapted from the Play by Edmond Rostand*. London: Faber & Faber.

Crimp, M. (2019c) *Lessons in Love and Violence*, in Crimp, M. *Writing for Nothing*. London: Faber & Faber, pp. 191–232.

Crimp, M. (2019d) *Men Asleep*, in Crimp, M. *The Hamburg Plays*. London: Faber & Faber, pp. 85–146.

Crimp, M. (2019f) 'The Play', in Crimp, M. *Writing for Nothing*. London: Faber & Faber, pp. 3–39.

Crimp, M. (2019g) *The Rest Will Be Familiar to You from Cinema*, in Crimp, M. *The Hamburg Plays*. London: Faber & Faber, pp. 1–84.

Crimp, M. (2019i) *When We Have Sufficiently Tortured Each Other: Twelve Variations on Samuel Richardson's Pamela*. London: Faber & Faber.

Crimp, M. (2019j) *Writing for Nothing*. London: Faber & Faber.

Oxford English Dictionary. (2021a) 'Desire, n.' Access provided by Mid Sweden University. Available at: https://www-oed-com.proxybib.miun.se/view/Entry/50880?rskey=z1EYoK&result=1&isAdvanced=false#eid (Accessed: 7 Dec. 2021).

Oxford English Dictionary. (2021b) 'Intertextuality, n.' Access provided by Mid Sweden University. Available at: https://www-oed-com.proxybib.miun.se/view/Entry/240987?redirectedFrom=intertextuality+&print (Accessed: 7 Dec. 2021).

Oxford English Dictionary. (2021c) 'Sexuality, n.' Access provided by Mid Sweden University. Available at: https://www-oed-com.proxybib.miun.se/view/Entry/177087?redirectedFrom=sexuality#eid (Accessed: 7 Dec. 2021).

Weeks, J. (2011) *The Languages of Sexuality*. London: Routledge.

1 Imitating Art

Fiction Pieces and Short Plays

However successful his theatre, Martin Crimp's writing has never been about one genre alone, from his early days as an author, to the more recent years that have produced a wider diversification of his output, particularly evident through his opera work. In 2019, the publication, as a collection, of *Writing for Nothing*, which holds together Crimp's opera texts, fiction, as well as shorter plays, consolidated the existence of this other, sometimes less visible, body of work. It would be inaccurate to propose that this has existed in parallel, because it has been developing in an intersecting way with the primary narrative of Crimp's playwriting. What *Writing for Nothing*, titled to wink at Samuel Beckett's *Stories and Texts for Nothing* (1967) (but perhaps also reminiscent of Harold Pinter's 'Writing for Myself' (1961)), accomplished was not only that it brought what might have otherwise been thought of as disparate mixed-genre texts together, presented to the reader in a way that might encourage their optimal exploration, but, also, that it rendered present what might have been previously overlooked. I hope that more academic work might be carried out specifically on Crimp as prose writer as well as, of course, as opera writer. To examine *Writing for Nothing* exhaustively is not the remit of the present book, though it would be an oversight not to engage with the volume selectively with the purpose of furnishing greater analytical depth. This would also help us better contextualize Crimp's work more broadly. There is a relationship and also, sometimes, a tension, between these sets of texts. The writer's voice is both distinctive throughout, and different.

Writing for Nothing features two texts described as *Writing in Prose*: 'The Play' and 'Stage Kiss', of which this chapter will be concentrating on the former, having discussed the latter in an earlier monograph in the context of *The Treatment*, along which it was originally published (1993). *Writing for Nothing* features seven texts under the *Writing for Theatre* section, of which I will be primarily engaging with *The Art*

DOI: 10.4324/9781003033400-2

of Painting, which most speaks to the thematic concerns of this book. The final section, *Writing for Opera*, includes Crimp's three opera texts; having discussed the earlier pieces (*Into the Little Hill* and *Written on Skin*) in previous work, here I will be concentrating on *Lessons in Love and Violence*, in the respective chapter.

'The Play', or Unravelling the Narrative(s) of Self

Crimp's longer-form short story (running at thirty-six pages) is significant and highly relevant to the context of this book, because it captures the author's engagement with intertextuality, with gender power politics and with irritative – and irritable – marriages equally. When the text begins, we are thrust into an action that has just taken place, and which concerns the story's eponymous event: the play. This specific play proves to be a moment unto itself – it delivers a break and a fissure of the visceral kind. As the story's narrator, a writer named John, tells us, 'When I heard the play read, it turned my stomach, but later that night I couldn't stop thinking about it' (2019f: 3). In an accomplished 'art-in-life' manoeuvre, in the following pages Crimp shows us how the event of the reading of the play in the theatre, amongst a team of professionals asked to provide feedback, which might, in any other context, have been deemed a mostly tepid occasion due to its relative ordinariness, rattles the principal narrator so considerably that his life begins to unravel. This includes his life in art, as an author and trusted member of the specific theatre's inner ecology, and his everyday life, that is, his marriage, which comes with its own tentative biorhythm. In terms of reading the story, matters are complicated further as the play that 'The Play' talks about, with its plot extremities and images of sexual violence in a relationship that appears largely non-consensual between two unequal partners, a powerful older man and a vulnerable young woman, is clearly reminiscent of Sarah Kane's *Blasted*. Kane's play, as is well documented, opened at the Royal Court in 1995, met with gendered aggression and in some cases outright hostility by several – overwhelmingly white, male, middle-aged – theatre critics, who, at the time, represented a social group as dominant as we might conceive of, against a newly emerging, young, female writer.

The 'art-in-life' concept that Crimp explores in 'The Play' runs deep: there is the matter of the young author, Rachel, representing an entirely different attitude to art – and life – from the narrator's own, even though they are colleagues, not least sharing the same venue, which – on the surface at least – values them both, albeit in different ways. Where she is unapologetic and prepared to clash with the system, which, on the other hand, appears ready to embrace her, he is compliant and reliable; where she is clearly headed for a major premiere event, his work has never received such attention, that we can gather from the story; where her work is irreverent and eccentric, his is prosaic and familiar. The author's frustration at the encounter with the young writer and her play is not the only element that leads to his irritability. There is also the matter of sudden confrontation with such wild narrative imagination, propelling the author to confront his own lack of boldness, whether in his safe career, or his comfortable marriage to Madeleine.

Specifically, even though the entire life/career narrative arc has been built on sturdy structural devices, and while its output has been predictable, it has never been exhilarating. Beyond a mid-life existential crisis, in an intertextual twist that is significant, the author begins to revisit his narrative, aware of the devices – the foundational compromises – that he deployed for its creation, so that it becomes exposed as the construct that it is. It is a construct that might, now, as unruliness has been injected in the everyday, fall apart, on account of the same principle that has hitherto allowed it to thrive: convenience. As the writer revisits his life's story, concentrating on moments that were as pivotal as they were mundane in punctuating his experience, he grows more aware of the underlying reality of its shortcomings. Matters come to a head when his existential crisis escalates, as he forces himself to face the fact that he simply could not tell as great a story as he had desired, or needed to; that the viability – and indeed performability – of his life has hinged on safe choices, which have, in fact, ended up being entirely unsafe. Hence, it is these same choices that will not suffice, in the current moment of reckoning, to shield him from personal and artistic exposure.

The more Crimp's writer narrativizes his life, intervening between reality and himself as an 'artful voyeur' (Heaney 2001: 31), the more he fails to locate himself firmly within it as a character. The realist tone of the short story, where the narrator engages in considerable in-depth encounters with psychologies and behaviours, differs from the often surrealist, often absurdist tone in which the break between individual and character – the incongruous make-up of a persona – that we encounter in, especially, later Crimp plays (for example, *Fewer Emergencies*; *The City*; *In the Republic of Happiness*) tends to unfold. Still, the seeds for the quest towards establishing the profound inner tension, while asking how the self is perceived and perceivable by others, how our narrative is written by those who engage with it, and how we may be categorized by our peers and by history, are present here in an intriguing way. Through the short story, Crimp gives us backstage access to the turmoil that several of his plays deal with as status quo for their protagonists (especially, perhaps, Clair in *The City*). In this case, we witness it in action, both in its causes and its outbursts.

John oscillates between versions of himself as he understands them, and versions of himself as understood by multiple others – his wife (in Crimp's familiar intertextual recycling of names, Madeleine is also the name of a major character in *In the Republic of Happiness*); his parents; her father; the theatre director who undercuts his authority; the irreverent young writer; as well as multiple theatre and industry figures, as the story adopts a not immediately detectable, but, rather, intricately woven in, shift of time and place, following intersecting episodic structures. 'The Play' is a sleight of hand of a text, because it is written by a playwright about the world of the theatre, retaining a relationship to people and events – or what we might deem to be such – that is just about close, or specific enough, for the reader to be tempted to consider the text a veiled reference. Although 'The Play' is not a play, and therefore the structure of the text and its storytelling operate under entirely different formal and stylistic conventions, Crimp's resistance to surrendering the meaning, or tying the narrative too resolutely to actuality persists. Therefore, even though the premise of 'The Play' is reminiscent of actual facts enough to lure us into a game of guessing, Crimp's upsetting of expectations ensures that the text accomplishes something entirely different. In a context of recent waves of public testimony regarding female subjugation in the arts, and indeed more broadly, by authoritarian male figures in professional contexts, as well as in everyday life, the short story could not be more topical. Under the ruse of a main event driven by a woman Crimp exposes the underlying narrative, the thread that holds together the systemic structures, and that is as fragile as it might appear firmly rooted: institutional male mediocrity and the voraciousness with which it clings to power, whether we take this to mean the director who commissions the play, or Crimp's primary narrator. Even though the former appears entirely arrogant and confident and the latter suffers from wavering self-confidence, these are both, in fact, the manifestations of the same desire: marking one's territory. As Crimp shows us here, desire is not necessarily, or, at least, not only and primarily sexual. Desire is also a matter of power distribution.

The way in which male mediocrity runs through art and life in this short story connects it to concerns that this book will explore further when the discussion turns to *Men Asleep*, where Crimp delivers ruminations so powerful into the deep-rooted causes of this state and its explosive repercussions that the effect is shattering. The fact that 'The Play', published in 2019, encourages us to return to dialogues that occurred in

1995, sealing a young female playwright's reputation in a way that has forever marked her narrative given her untimely death, accomplishes a twofold task. Firstly, it allows a new readership, to whom the events surrounding the premiere of Kane's *Blasted* may not be (fully) known given the time that has now elapsed, the opportunity to trace the thread and appreciate the historicity of systemic oppressions and true struggles that the recent movements of #MeToo and #TimesUp have revealed: namely, that male entitlement has always been an institutional trope blocking women's (equal) access. Secondly, it exposes male opportunism – whether in the shape of the director who commissions the play without considering essential structures of care towards the fledgling playwright (who will become the target of attacks and aggression), or in the shape of the playwright, who feels that their own identity is becoming threatened by the importance of someone younger, and potentially more gifted, though he chooses a passive-aggressive way of performing his resistance.

The artist's vulnerability, then, emerges as a tangible concern, as does the inevitable comparison between oneself and one's peers within the theatre domain and its arising web of relationships. In 'The Play', Crimp shows us that both conditions are likely to become amplified when the artist at the heart of the story is female, because the systems in place are ill-equipped to support her, but, also, because in a male-dominated field, her talent causes her to become more conspicuous, more exposed. The critique of such attitudes strikes me as strong and resolute despite the otherwise discreet tone and nature of the piece. John, then, is equally concerned as to the inadequacy of protective structures (or, rather, their lack) and riddled with their inner workings, from which he has benefited. 'The Play' confronts the gradual moulding of the male artist into a passive force that enjoys own privileges without being ready, or willing, to share these with others – especially with those that have been chronically sidelined. Such are the complexities of Crimp's piece: it provides us with a narrator that exhibits both tenderness and cruelty, however veiled.

With jealousy intruding increasingly, whether because Madeleine, the relative failure of whose acting career has always provided a degree of soothing comfort for John, has now been cast in the irreverent new play, or because the young playwright is about to experience attention greater than he ever has, as the text allows us to gauge, the narrator's artistic and personal shortcomings come to a head. I would like, here, to consider relevant investigations of couple dynamics with particular reference to the performances involved in maintaining a given marriage ecology. As researchers have proposed:

working well together suggests a coordination of effort and may often require that each partner develop and maintain a unique set of performance niches within the relationship. [...] The web of interconnected factors that supports the development of special-ized performance niches by each partner might be termed the couple's performance ecology [...which] exists within every com-mitted, romantic relationship; that the set of performance niches occupied by each partner and the relative performance of partners within their respective niches provide a context for understanding marital processes.

(Beach, Tesser, Mendolia, Anderson, Crelia, Whitaker, and Fincham 1996: 379)

At this stage in 'The Play', we are about to witness what transpires when performance niches, or, what others have called 'role perfor-mance' (Schafer and Braito 1979: 802), and, along with these, 'the cou-ple's performance ecology' become disrupted. As has additionally been noted, it is essential to have 'recognition of the role played by one's own or one's partner's outstanding performance and the concomitant emotions of pride in one's partner, contempt for one's partner, pride in oneself, and shame-envy that may intrude on married life from time to time' (Beach, Tesser, Mendolia, Anderson, Crelia, Whitaker, and Fincham 1996: 380). Moreover, 'any theory of teamwork should lead to the prediction that feelings of pride in one's partner or contempt for one's partner should be related to how well partners coordinate their performance niches' (Beach, Tesser, Mendolia, Anderson, Crelia, Whitaker, and Fincham 1996: 380). At this moment in 'The Play', 'per-formance niches' become unhinged; implicit 'teamwork' is exposed as mere enabling and 'shame-envy' prevails. Personal and professional worlds intersect and, beyond this, collide with sudden force in ways that may appear unforeseen, but, also, may strike us as thoroughly inev-itable; a crisis long overdue.

In one case we read that Madeleine confronts John, saying '[...] you're jealous. Of me and of her [Rachel]. Meaning you don't want me to succeed. Or anyone to succeed. You're so full of hate. Why are you so full of hate?' (36). In another extract, John admits: 'Normally if a young writer was discussing with the Director [Crimp's capitalization of the word is reminiscent of *Four Imaginary Characters*, the prose/short story introduction pieces to the first volume of his collected plays, of which 'The Director' is one] and myself the reading of their first play, she'd be looking for reassurance and advice. We'd feel a gratifying sense of responsibility and power' (5). As John realizes, however, the state of play, as it were, is now different: he has been rendered irrelevant, and it is the director that is effusive in gratitude, rather than the young writer. John's irrelevance concerns not only his artistic scrutiny, which appears, if not cancelled out, then, certainly, sidelined, but, also, his quiet authority as partner – unable to prevent his wife from accepting the role. Just as Madeleine refuses to validate him as a counsel, so Rachel shows no desire of acknowledging him as a mentor.

The above-cited quotations open up to a broader issue that *Men Asleep* also homes in on with sharpness and precision: the veiled aggression that stems from men unable to match, or indeed even tolerate, the success of women, despite all apparent quotidian performances of support. References to marriage as performance more broadly begin early in 'The Play' and continue to land with considerable frequency throughout, as do references to the self as performer. Early on, John describes himself as momentarily 'feeling like a badly written character, not sure of my intentions' (6). Narratives may be built gradually, but their collapse can be swift and spectacular:

> Everyone creates and maintains a personal narrative that may be essential to his or her sense of personal continuity but that is nonetheless subject to revision and elaboration (Greenwald, 1980). [...R]elationship narratives likewise may play an important role in maintaining couple stability or at least in predicting couple dissolution (Buehlman et al., 1992). [...C]ouple narratives may be subject to revision and elaboration in response to motivational factors (Baumeister, Wortman, & Stillwell, 1993; Vaughn, 1990).
> (Beach, Tesser, Mendolia, Anderson, Crelia, Whitaker, and Fincham 1996: 382)

Crimp's writing illuminates this state of being both in terms of the individual's relationship to themselves, in the matter of teleological self-perception, and of interaction with others, including existing within interpersonal – sometimes intimate – structures. Marriage is, it follows, one of these, and it often emerges as the by-default challenging condition within which to define one's 'character', and, by extension, one's role.

We witness this state as problematic and ultimately debilitating in *The City*, where Clair fails to write the story of either herself or those around her, or of a successful marriage, whether emotionally or financially, eventually surrendering the narrative. 'The Play' offers a more mundane depiction of this struggle, and more formally conventional, though no less complex. The sense of marriage as performance is accentuated further by John's constant framing of expectations when it comes to anticipating Madeleine's reactions, or to interpreting her actions, similarly to how he frames his own typical responses to familiar triggers. It becomes apparent that the couple are complicit performers well accustomed to their patterns, collaborating like scene partners rather than anything more profound. Everything in John and Madeleine's life is staged, and intentional: from the clutter in their comfortable home to the way in which their role balance ensures that he is the more practical of the two, a trait which is compatible with his overall reliability as a writer for the theatre he collaborates with, while she is more impetuous. The fact that Madeleine's father is a theatre producer, one whose career was built on staging commercial shows placating audiences as comfort viewing, adds yet another layer of theatricality: his generous gift of a house, the very set for John and Madeleine's marriage, serves, in a way, as the building of a production – he is the patron in all possible senses.

When John recalls an episode in their life where he and Madeleine must decide whether or not they will accept her father's sizeable gift, he describes a scene that he will dub 'Our country-house melodrama' (9) on the basis of the humdrum, 'safe' amount of conflict, both internal and towards each other, that the two are experiencing. In what is a major moment for the marriage, leading to a sense of literal and symbolic indebtedness, and so, a turning point in the plot of the relationship, John sees the exchange around the negotiation as already tired, even though it is relatively early days: 'I hope our dialogue wasn't that stilted, but I suspect it was' (8). How he continues is all the more telling concerning Crimp's insightful look at the delicate balances involved in the crafting of a marriage, including the right amount of tolerable cruelty that distinguishes its protagonists on a daily basis: 'It's only years of marriage that have honed our conversations into something altogether more subtle and hurtful', he observes (8). The verbal choreography, the physicality and precision that is embedded in the sharpness of language and the agility through which speech and bodies swerve around perceived risk so as to continue – and to prevail – is a game for two partners. Taken too far, matters slip outside of control and risk rises: it is a process that Crimp explores more explicitly in *Men Asleep* and in *When We Have Sufficiently Tortured Each Other*. In a way, both these plays offer the embodiment of danger at the stretching – and trespassing – of tacitly acknowledged boundaries, when one of the two partners, or, sometimes, both together, considering whether to tempt risk, or to engage with it consciously as a tantalizing element, choose to take one step further than the previously designated zone of play.

Beyond such moments of revelation, or confrontation, the linguistic palette of 'The Play' is such that words are interwoven throughout in a way that communicates the reality of marriage as a setup, both in the sense of a construct, and in the sense of a confining structure in which two individuals willingly enter, and to which they commit. The commitment itself bears nothing idealistic. Oftentimes it is perseverance for the enterprise not to fail as a mode of self-preservation and a sustainable character storyline that appears to drive the effort when facing the prospect of, say, the collapsed narrative of *The City* and all the consequences of a failed marriage. Conditioning is key: after all, 'one of the factors related to the evaluation of a spouse's performance in marital roles is the marriage partner's self-concept and the marriage partner's perception of the spouse's evaluation of him/her' (Schafer and Braito 1979: 802; the gender binary pronouns are reflective of the time in which the article was written). Characters behave, and adapt, as fit within given parameters – in 'The Play' phrases such as 'the whole frame of my feelings' (9), which, for John, Madeleine occupies at the start of their relationship, further reveal marriage as construct, but, also, the partner's sphere of influence.

The way in which, doubly as an actor, Madeleine takes on the role of the wife to adapt to the expectations of John's parents, themselves both geographically and socially entirely remote from the couple's lifestyle, 'pretending to be *the girl-next-door*' (14, my emphasis; here we may be reminded of the eponymous scenario of the accessibly-packaged entertainment figure in *Attempts on Her Life*), or, also, the way in which John never entirely feels – at least in terms of class – the equal of Madeleine, confessing to the reader that at times he 'look[s] like a character from the past – the servant' (32), a likely cross-reference to Madeleine's most important career role, her turn in a Strindberg production, are further hints. This time, we glimpse at the casting that has tacitly taken place between them, changing on the basis of who the 'extras' are that enter the playing field of the marriage on an everyday basis, what behavioural adjustments they require, and how these impact, in a subtle or more dramatic way, the ecology of the couple. In another example, when Madeleine is cast in Rachel's play, causing a spectacular fight between her and John, she is observed, through his writer's gaze, as 'performing the most extraordinary movement' (36), adding to the physical drama of the confrontation in a way that is wholly theatrical. John, narrativizing and processing the options available to him in terms of his next moves in the fight, registers that it is Madeleine who decides how to 'set up the scene' (38) so as to limit the range of his possible reactions, assuming he is looking to avoid what, by placing it in quotation marks,

Crimp's narrator alerts us to as meta-reference, the phrase heard before, the played out plot twist: John's perceived "'brutality'" (38). And, so, John is disallowed from entering the room where Madeleine is, and, by extension, unable 'to play back to her the look on her face' (39) as he so desires. The narrated marriage conflict is an intertextual engagement with the source narrative: the marriage itself. Everything is script.

The specific extract, leading us to the finale of the story, which closes as the couple are still engaged in a fight, notably makes reference to the way in which the couple physically move from one part of their house to another and the house itself becomes a coercive force, as in other work by Crimp, where homes carry the burden of the problematic relationships they accommodate in an embodied, inhabited way, an equal partner in the dysfunction. *The Country* is, arguably, the most characteristic example, though such instances abound, to a greater or lesser extent, across Crimp's oeuvre. The house in 'The Play' is a form of set: there are references to its objects, not least to transient ones, props from an everyday life. So when Crimp closes the story in the following words, with John surveying the field after the fight, and revealing the explosive rage that has sent objects flying, we know to read beyond the level of realist observation of everyday detail. The fight has had casualties – so we learn from John: 'I rescue the bills [on the kitchen table]: the bills have survived. But the play is covered in jam and fragments of glass, and is beyond saving' (39). In the last words of the text, lies everything. The staples of ordinariness – in an intelligent nod, particularly, to the capitalist tropes, the lowest and most resistant common denominator of finances – endure; but the play of the marriage may have entered a new act, whose outcome is uncertain. The play that is smothered in debris is, on a literal level, Rachel's script, as a physical entity, paper destroyed by liquid. But there is also the content, and the structure of the play, that John has always evaluated as problematic, that we might read as a reference here. Once more Rachel's play serves as a meta-theatrical reference for the relationship itself: John and Madeleine's setup of a marriage is also beyond saving – the 'fragments of glass' have cut through to the core; the violence has prevailed; the nucleus is soiled, penetrated, shattered.

Beyond the meta-theatrical element stemming from John and Madeleine's respective professions, as well as from the crisis catalyst of Rachel's play, in 'The Play' there are also important intertextual references to Crimp's other work. These serve to create an overall atmosphere of self-reflexive irony for the story and its different characters, who appear to share the fact that they find themselves in existential crossroads against a climate of purported self-betterment. Such a feeling is captured in comments such as 'Things are improving, oh yes' (22), which may remind the reader of the respective repeated lines in *Fewer Emergencies* and which John thinks to himself as he takes a break from a meeting in the theatre to catch up with his own sense of a world suddenly closing in, which is manifesting as strong physical discomfort. But there is also the matter of one of the most persistent themes: the broken intimacy between married couples that resounds in its absence, attempted, demanded, denied, suspended. In Crimp, this materializes often in the shape of resistance to that supposedly simplest gesture of tenderness: the kiss between two partners. It is a resistance cruel and purposeful, as much as it is an inadvertent and unavoidable response to the request of a jaded partner equally disinvested in an act, whose performance they are merely wielding as a form of power-play. In 'The Play', occurrences land when John reminisces as to how Madeleine once interrupted a conversation that was beginning to turn towards the couple's finances to say: 'I want you to kiss me' (31), which echoes another moment that John will narrate later, when Madeleine interrupts another awkward conversation to demand of John: 'I expect you to kiss me', to which he replies: 'What if I don't want to kiss you?' (34).

In Crimp's work, the withholding of a kiss is meaningful – particularly hurtful and, beyond that, passive-aggressively vindictive; a form of x-ray for a couple's innermost state, which can, otherwise, become obscured in words. Examples of particular relevance concern Corinne and Richard in *The Country*, where a suspended kiss marks the finale of the play, or Clair and Chris in *The City*, where the artificiality of the marriage absolutely intervenes against any genuine intimacy. The short story 'Stage Kiss', moreover, elevates the act to an entire plot-line, exploring the absence of real emotion vis-à-vis stage construct. It is important that when John, earlier in 'The Play', runs into Rachel outside a pub, she kisses him on the cheek – 'not a theatre-kiss, but a real one in which her lips touch my skin' (26), as he observes, and one that later John will admit to 'still feel[ing] [...] on my skin, like a dab of ether' (27). Such a kiss is the one not given between Crimp's couples; it is the kind of fleeting kiss too real and impactful for the stilted, staged relationships that so often compose these matrimonial arrangements; it is also the opposite of 'Stage Kiss' where the actor narrator describes the kiss he exchanges with his fellow performer as 'violent, technical, prolonged' (46), a calculated intensity that is otherwise entirely lacking from his life. Yet, it is the experience of that life, as he shares with us, that has helped inform the very technique that goes into making the stage kiss realistic – a performance that is repeated nightly with the spectators having 'No inkling of deceit' (47). The theatrically performed kiss is present because the real one is not – all truth has evaporated to serve art, and art is the only thing that endures, as real as life itself, and just the same amount of artificial, too.

The intertextuality in Crimp's writing is far from confined to literary texts – including Crimp's own – because it emerges equally sharply through the engagement with the narratives of other artists, which may not be word-based at all. On some occasions this is music; on others it is painting. In 'The Play', as John is imagining the contours of his life with Madeleine, the parameters in which it materializes and the canvas on which it plays out, he finds himself thinking of Edvard Munch and his desolate figures against a backdrop both pervasive and irrelevant to the drama between the two bodies drifting apart from one another. John's memory registers Madeleine's 'hair hung down her back like a curtain of black, brown and gold, excluding me' (9). 'We might've looked like a woodcut by Munch' (9), he muses. But it cannot be, because the high drama of the painting proves too much for the pale reproduction that reality offers for it – if only 'it hadn't been Berkshire' (9), John adds. Real life, then, is never but a poor, lacking excuse for the high drama of art – its canvasses demand greatness, but the everyday is a mere replica, and, as such, must dispense with grandeur by default. The settings of well-worn relationships and their established dynamics, the only preserver of otherwise tentative bonds, are captured affectively by Crimp across different genres of work. Real life might imitate, but can never quite match the intensity of art. Art, on the contrary, has the capacity to expose real life's nakedness, proving it thin and unsatisfactory, as power shifts play out in scenes that, but for the characters' own sense of self-importance in their power struggles, otherwise lack monumentality.

The Artful Intersection

Monumentality itself can be found in high art, with which Crimp engages often, probing, sometimes, the moment in which the encounter of art with the mundane might serve as an attempt to elevate it, infusing a certain intensity, which, however, only seems to burn briefly before it evaporates. Such a moment is captured in the short-form, breathless narrative pace of *The Art of Painting*. As concerns style and rhythm, this condensed theatre piece seizes the exhilaration of encounter with the globally revered masterpiece and the attempt to translate it through words, while, at the same time, revealing why any attempt will, ultimately, prove fruitless and inadequate. *The Art of Painting* is a text that deftly exposes systemic patriarchal jurisdiction over art, while, at the same time, diffusing and even ridiculing it through a master-class of linguistic dexterity. In other words, the topic of the text is what, today, we might describe as 'mansplaining': a male-identifying individual's assumption of unwarranted authority in instructing others, especially non-male, how to think, interpret or engage with any situation or stimulus. With a first logged usage in 2008 as indicated in the *Oxford English Dictionary* (2021c; under 'mansplain'), the term, both transitive and intransitive (capturing the mere incidental perception of any other entity given the assumption of authority in the subject himself), is defined as 'Of a man: to explain (something) needlessly, overbearingly, or condescendingly, esp. (typically when addressing a woman) in a manner thought to reveal a patronizing or chauvinistic attitude' (2021c). Such are the concerns that *The Art of Painting* unpacks in its brief, yet rich in information, narrative body, building the ideal context for the exposition and condemnation of the social phenomenon: the voluntary encounter with the artwork, which produces, for the narrator, a further encounter with an overbearing stranger – this one involuntary.

In their edited volume *Museum Activism* (2019), Robert R. Janes and Richard Sandell focus on 'the inherent and inevitably political character of museums' stemming from 'the narratives they construct and disseminate, as well as the part these narratives play in shaping our collective understanding of difference, fairness and equality' (8). The dissemination occurs through curation; through the modes of encounter that are facilitated; but, also, through the encouraging, or dismantling, of dominant narratives regarding the engagement with the artwork itself. This is the range that Crimp's *The Art of Painting* is concerned with, against any form of discrimination; against exclusion, whether aggressively or passively performed. 'The museum must now become an institution of the commons – a resource belonging to and affecting the whole of a community' write Janes and Sandell (17). The same holds true of the iconic artwork, for which the museum provides a home, and which, as Crimp's text shows us, ought to constitute common property, presented and perceived in modes non-classist, non-gendered, non-ageist, non-privileged, non-sexist, and, ultimately, non-discriminatory in any form. Janes and Sandell propose: 'We know, as museum practitioners and academics, what we do, but most often we do not know what effects or results will ensue from what we do. [...] We are again in the territory of complexity theory, where chaos, non-linearity, emergence, and the loss of control are paramount' (18). The unruly narrative as captured by Crimp's witness/narrator reflects precisely this moment of emergence and disruption in dialogue with our present socio-political climate as regards women's rights and access (physical and conceptual), for which the encounter with the artwork of diachronic significance serves as prompt, proving its own unpredictability beyond any canonicity. New narratives, as Crimp's text shows us, can be superscribed at any stage, and what great artworks share is that their significance may alter as new social narratives emerge, and old, dysfunctional ones are contested. Here, the artwork becomes the site for both the performance of extant chauvinist narratives and their exposition as ridiculous. The museum itself emerges as space of intersections and crossings, in which no single perspective carries more authority than another, because, to quote Gaston Bachelard, the museum ought to serve as 'protective space' (1994: xxxv).

The reference to intersectionality in the title of this sub-section speaks to the fact that the text also captures the ways in which such a power play, beyond classed and privileged, is also intensely gendered, serving as an unwelcome overture from a man towards a woman. In turn, this results in an infringement of space both public (the museum) and personal (one's own territory in which the corporeal encounter of the artwork occurs), which borders on, if not directly constitutes, harassment. Art historian Griselda Pollock asserts: 'What we conceptualise as art is a moment of creative difference, difference as the shock of creative differentiation whose sources are not universal. The nature of the differentiation becomes radical according to the hegemony of the dominant mode of systematicity, in our case, of phallocentric, heteronormative, bourgeois, globalising capitalism' (2011). In *The Art of Painting*, Crimp appears to be investigating the patrimonial hegemonic narratives that have long promoted the male beholder as an authority when it comes to asserting knowledge over art, rendering it yet another gendered power trope. Pollock continues: 'Interpretation is [...] not the application of a pre-given system to an artwork in order to maintain its function as the support of the system. It is the engagement with the working, the economy of a complex material, intellectual, sensuous, affective and social practice in which a medium functions as an intermediary screen between subjects generating a moment of potential trans-subjectivity' (2011). In order to elicit this moment of 'trans-subjectivity', the encounter itself ought to be dialectical and intertextual, the beholder's narrative interacting with the artwork. The account of the event that forms the narrative spine of *The Art of Painting* is given to us by the person to whom the figure that dominates the narrative – the man standing next to them looking at the artwork – speaks. They act as a vessel and refractor for this man's thoughts, physicality, and overall transgression. By relaying these to the reader, the narrator captures

the precise hegemonic structures that hinder the democracy of interpretation, that fracture trans-subjectivity, and that render the moment
non-dialectical.

The artwork that serves as trigger and site for the unfolding of Crimp's
narrative is the eponymous one that lends the short text its name:
Vermeer's *The Art of Painting* (1666/68); also known as *The Allegory of
Painting*. This alternative rendition of the title is one that Crimp's text
appears particularly attuned to, given that it deploys the painting as
an allegory, a visual vehicle and interpretative and spatial framework
around which the episode it presents to the spectator unfolds. *The Art of
Painting* accomplishes a great deal for a text this short, proving Crimp's
ability to generate depth irrespective of length. The maximalism lies in
expression and the reach of words rather than explanation, as the piece
only runs for two and a half pages of printed text. In it, Crimp manages to introduce us, also, to the context in which his speaker/narrator
finds themselves sharing the artwork. Neither city [Vienna] nor cultural institution [Kunsthistorisches Museum] are named, though this is
the venue where Vermeer's painting is held, and, also, where Crimp's
piece was first performed in 2015. Further elements contributing to site
contextualization concern references to the city's socio-political past
and present. The age of the city, and specifically its endurance and
transition, only add to the existential angst of the transgressive male
speaker, who is aware of his fading relevance. Moreover, the past with
its artistic and historical urtexts looms heavily, augmenting both the
man's attempts to reassert it and his aggressiveness towards a younger
generation. Such aggression is as gendered as it is motivated by a sense
of lack, the greatness of the painting serving as reflector of the man's
own insufficiencies. As the piece progresses, it captures the man's desperate realization that the woman, who will not engage with him in
any way he might desire, or pay heed to his self-assumed authority,
occupies a space from which he is forever excluded.

Even though the text never directly reveals much about the narrator,
Crimp's overall prioritization of the female perspective and experience
in his work, as well as his consistent engagement with and exposure of
the systemic structures that entrap women in problematic frameworks
aiding and abating toxic masculinities, allow us to deduce that it is a
younger woman, who has found herself in the path of an older man's
self-indulgent monologue, as he attempts to interfere with her agency.
Supporting such a hypothesis is the following quoted extract:

> Yes, he said, the Art of Painting, one of my favourite pictures,
> I come here to lose myself, he said, whatever I mean by lose myself,

lose myself in the light, lose myself, he said to me, in the blue and
gold. Yes when you think of all the shit that passes for art now,
and the people, he said, who raise it up, […] unless I should blame
someone like you, he said to me, since young people have no roots,
[…] and they only enter galleries like this to take photographs on
their phones or buy postcards […].

(Crimp 2019a: 111)

As the monologue, mediated by the narrator, continues, revealing the
man's privileged saturation and emotional discontent, the fact that
Crimp provides a mere seven full-stops in the entire text reveals the
narrator's own perception of the torrential, non-sequitur speech, whose
uninvited force she encounters. When the man does pause for breath,
it is to ask questions:

Why won't you speak to me? he said. Is it because I'm a man? Is
it because I'm old? Is it because I'm close to death while you still
stand at an unimaginable distance from it like the young girl in this
painting?

(113)

What follows is an act of self-extrication from the narratives of other
men, whose attitude, as the narrator informs us, this man berates,
describing them in profoundly unflattering terms that all converge
upon the same kind of self-importance. Even though it is precisely this
trait that he is displaying himself, he continues to take a myopic view
to the fact, proclaiming himself different from

the kind of man, he said, who, unlike me, he said, imagines a
woman's job is simply to listen and to redeem, has no interest in
her inner life or intellectual attainments, sees this or indeed any
woman's silence as a vacuum his words are obliged to fill, the kind
of man who cannot even for one moment imagine, he said, how
the light must glow behind her half-closed eyes.

(113)

This very verbal sequence, which closes the text, also exposes the problem: men who have systemically thought themselves superior to gender
oppression; who fail, like John in 'The Play', to recognize that they are
part of the problem, believing themselves noble.

As the artwork – no less, by a male artist – depicts a painter, his back
turned to the spectator, in the early stages of capturing the image of a

woman, whose gaze he will not know, nor 'how the light must glow behind her half-closed eyes', because she is instructed to forever (at least in spectatorial time) face downwards, so that this woman is rendered doubly by a male perspective, so the scene repeats in real life. That is, a young woman is instructed by an older man on the value of art, and what it ought to be. Intertextualities, intentional or spontaneous – depending on how we might interpret the narrative of this encounter – are also a form of proliferating the shortcomings of the canon, Crimp's text seems to be suggesting. The achievement of Crimp's piece in the final section quoted above is remarkable, because it accomplishes several forms of impact at the same time. Firstly, it exposes the obliviousness in men's transgressions against women, even as they are perpetrating them – in this case by invading personal space and releasing a form of attack, packaged as instruction. Secondly, by probing how the male gaze in its different iterations has been dominant through structures in place that have facilitated it for centuries, in art and in life, the text also reveals how women have – often silently, yet no less critically – both absorbed and processed this to its tiniest minutiae. Finally, there is the fact that the young woman, as she records the man's monologue, creates a form of dialogue between real life and artwork, as she, herself, is now reflected in the woman in the painting – her act of profound engagement with this moment, the painting, the man, a mere layer in the overall complexity of her experience, 'the light behind [… her own] half-closed eyes', which is irreducible to the male beholder's pronouncements.

There is, therefore, a strong meta-referential and intertextual element in Crimp's *The Art of Painting*, whose very title is such. With this text, Crimp delivers the double gesture of highlighting the artwork, while, at the same time, creating a vehicle for critique of entrenched gendered attitudes towards the interpretation of art, in a way most helpful towards posing the question of who serves, after all, as art's keeper, and how the institutional space ought to provide access, but, also, to care and preserve. The latter concerns both the artwork, and the female observer/agent, as she is neither an object, nor a vessel for men's claims to genius, but a presence and a force in herself. Given the fact that it is, also, the acts of staging and spectatorship within a broader cultural space and institutional context that Crimp's text addresses, it was especially important that, in 2019, as part of an event marking the span of Crimp's career in the broader context of the National Theatre's production of *When We Have Sufficiently Tortured Each Other*, and as *Writing for Nothing* had just been published, *The Art of Painting* was the piece that Crimp chose to read before the audience.[1]

Closing Reflections

The anthological nature of *Writing for Nothing* allows themes that relate to sexual and gendered tension, repression, oppression, and suppression to emerge particularly strongly and from different angles. No world is safe: not that of the domestic, or of art, or of citizenship, or of politics, as transgressions intersect into hyper-crises. The intertext itself, allowing the space of intersection that it also generates, is a particularly fruitful literary means of revealing and capturing the issue, without claiming to resolve it. Texts like *Party*, for example, a short play premiered by the Royal Court in June 2010 as part of its Elephant and Castle initiative, as the United Kingdom was transitioning to a Conservative-led Coalition government, playing on the ambiguity of the title word and echoing Harold Pinter's play *Party Time* (1991), taps precisely into the transgressive structures which the elite encourages, and on which it thrives. These are structures that embed violence by default: violence so pervasive that it is normalized, as Pinter's text, which stages a reception held by the privileged few while their regime is violently suppressing dissidents on the streets of the city outside, also shows us. The same proto-conservative principles are taken on in both the Crimp and the Pinter pieces: commitment to the cause (or the party); patriarchal domination; an implicit, and immediate threat against any deviation from the party line that might be – even inadvertently – expressed. As he does often, Crimp resists naming speakers in the dialogue. The text exposes the absurdity of incendiary power at the same time as delving into the frameworks that enable it. For example, the dialogue reads:

—— I really respect everyone's religion and especially when it involves a sex-crime – there's something about that kind of crime that makes good feelings resonate throughout the world.

[…]

—— I want to be there. I want to hold the knife. I want to smear the blood. I want to mix the cum with the blood.

[…]

—— You can – yes you can – the knife is yours – and so is the tender victim. Everyone wins.

(2019e: 56)

Crimp's text, therefore, takes on the absurdism of self-indulgent exclusionary power with caustic precision and clarity: this is a new world in which violations – political, sexual, financial, religious – are spoken about under the same breath as the so-called commitment to philanthropy and equality. Politics in its broadest spectrum is a game of power and desire at their darkest, this short play shows us. Crimp's exposition of cruelty too profound and resolute to become displaced and the razor-sharp depiction of the urges and entitlements that establish and promulgate such narratives, fosters the idea of a dialogue that is happening in spite of the majority of so-called active agents, or, perhaps, because of their subtle and successful manipulation. Another form of desire, as the text implies, is that which concerns exerting unequal authority over a pliable party that is lured in as partner, but, then, is proven to be merely a pawn. It is this manipulable base that becomes drawn into the narrative of those politically powerful, under the false conviction that one will be cared for, and looked after – a feeling not unlike a toxic attachment to an abusive partner.

In the work prioritized in this chapter the meta-element is predominant, and when it comes to representations of life in art, or life staged in the model of art, or life existing in the domain of art because of the characters' spatial and social contexts, then the situation becomes more complex still, and the relationships between texts – literary and/or visual – and reality are rendered dangerously fluid. At the root of it all, as we have seen in 'The Play', lies the profound need to question social norms especially in their so-called protective capacities, revealing that there is no such quality as a safe environment, no matter how settled, or privileged, or self-narrativized in one's – and one's partner's – predictability one might feel. Tacit exchanges of power are corrosive, and continuous; the structure of a home, like that of a text, can be eroded when exposed to external agents that attack the uncomfortable structures within, however comfortable in their guise these might at first appear. Such is the situation we encounter in one of Crimp's most recent, deceptively elliptical and startlingly deep-running texts, *Men Asleep*, which is the focus of the next chapter.

Note

1. The event 'Exploring Martin Crimp's Plays' took place on 15 February 2019 at the National Theatre, Cottesloe Room, Clore Learning Centre, and was led by Vicky Angelaki.

Bibliography

Bachelard, G. (1994) *The Poetics of Space*. Translated by M. Jolas. Boston: Beacon Press.

Beach, S. R. H., Tesser, A., Mendolia, M., Anderson, P., Crelia, R., Whitaker, D. and Fincham, F. D. (1996) 'Self-Evaluation Maintenance in Marriage: Toward a Performance Ecology of the Marital Relationship', *Journal of Family Psychology*, 10(4), pp. 379–396.

Beckett, S. (1967) *Stories and Texts for Nothing*. New York: Grove Press.

Crimp, M. (1993) *The Treatment*. London: Faber & Faber.

Crimp, M. (1997) *Attempts on Her Life*. London: Faber & Faber.

Crimp, M. (2000a) *The Country*. London: Faber & Faber.

Crimp, M. (2000b) *Four Imaginary Characters*, in *Martin Crimp: Plays One*. London: Faber & Faber.

Crimp, M. (2005a) *Fewer Emergencies*. London: Faber & Faber.

Crimp, M. (2008) *The City*. London: Faber & Faber.

Crimp, M. (2012b) *In the Republic of Happiness*. London: Faber & Faber.

Crimp, M. (2019a) *The Art of Painting*, in Crimp, M. *Writing for Nothing*. London: Faber & Faber, pp. 107–113.

Crimp, M. (2019c) *Lessons in Love and Violence*, in Crimp, M. *Writing for Nothing*. London: Faber & Faber, pp. 191–232.

Crimp, M. (2019d) *Men Asleep*, in Crimp, M. *The Hamburg Plays*. London: Faber & Faber, pp. 85–146.

Crimp, M. (2019e) *Party*, in Crimp, M. *Writing for Nothing*. London: Faber & Faber, pp. 51–60.

Crimp, M. (2019f) 'The Play', in Crimp, M. *Writing for Nothing*. London: Faber & Faber, pp. 3–39.

Crimp, M. (2019g) *The Rest Will Be Familiar to You from Cinema*, in Crimp, M. *The Hamburg Plays*. London: Faber & Faber, pp. 1–84.

Crimp, M. (2019h) 'Stage Kiss', in Crimp, M. *Writing for Nothing*. London: Faber & Faber, pp. 41–47.

Crimp, M. (2019i) *When We Have Sufficiently Tortured Each Other: Twelve Variations on Samuel Richardson's Pamela*. London: Faber & Faber.

Crimp, M. (2019j) *Writing for Nothing*. London: Faber & Faber.

Heaney, S. (2001) 'Punishment', in Heaney, S. *North*. London: Faber & Faber, pp. 30–31.

Janes, R. R. and Sandell, R. (eds.) (2019) *Museum Activism*. London: Routledge.

Kane, S. (2001) *Blasted*, in *Sarah Kane: Complete Plays*. London: Methuen Drama, pp. 1–61.

Oxford English Dictionary (2021c) 'Mansplain, v.' Access provided by Mid Sweden University. Available at: https://www-oed-com.proxybib.miun.se/view/Entry/59997929?redirectedFrom=mansplain&print (Accessed: 13 Dec. 2021).

Pinter, H. (1996) 'Introduction: Writing for Myself', in *Harold Pinter: Plays Two*. London: Faber & Faber, pp. vii–xi.

Pinter, H. (2012) *Party Time*, in *Harold Pinter: Plays Four*. London: Faber & Faber, pp. 279–314.

Pollock, G. (2011) 'What If Art Desires to Be Interpreted? Remodelling Interpretation after the 'Encounter-Event', *Tate Papers*, 15. Available at: https://www.tate.org.uk/research/publications/tate-papers/15/what-if-art-desires-to-be-interpreted-re-modelling-interpretation-after-the-encounter-event (Accessed: 21 Dec. 2021).

Schafer, R. B. and Braito, R. (1979) 'Self-Concept and Role Performance Evaluation Among Marriage Partners', *Journal of Marriage and Family*, 41(4), pp. 801–810.

Vermeer van Delft, J. (1666/68) *The Art of Painting*. [Oil on canvas]. Kunsthistorisches Museum, Vienna.

2 Mating for Life

Men Asleep

The painter Maria Lassnig (1919–2014), whose piece *Schlafende Männer* lends the title to Martin Crimp's play that, in turn, forms the primary reference of this chapter, tended to produce impactful, large-scale work; there is nothing discreet or subdued about Lassnig's tableaux, even if they often merely capture a moment of suspension: of the mind – in thought, or reverie – and of the body – before a major gesture, or reaction. The event, that is, becomes the build-up, rather than the action itself. The focus is placed on the monumentality in that indeterminate space between what preceded, and what will arrive next, the scene pregnant with possibilities, carrying the seed of a potentially major crisis. It is this aesthetics that particularly speaks to the contents of Crimp's play. By the time Lassnig settles into her distinctive colour palette of soft, even dreamlike hues, utterly clashing with the intensity of the paintings themselves (in expression; in theme), she has refined her craft to a distinctive style, wholly her own. As we might expect in a career that spans most of the twentieth century and stretches into the twenty-first, Lassnig travels through abstraction, surrealism and minimalism to land on maximalism, her work continuing to startle through its overture to encounter and confrontation: with the self; with another; with the world. These are paintings that mark a reckoning: one that is internal – it is, after all, always the subject's own journey that Lassnig appears to be concerned with – but one that has also, in that specific moment, been suddenly accelerated by an external stimulus.

Amidst the strangeness, wonder and pain that Lassnig's work often captures, and where she, herself, features regularly through the form of self-portrait, there is also a consistent tendency towards humour and sarcasm. On occasion, this is self-directed, without ever compromising the fact that the subject takes herself very seriously as sentient mind and body, and therefore as a site of agency for thoughts,

DOI: 10.4324/9781003033400-3

emotions, desires, and urges. But what Lassnig delivers so potently through her profoundly socially involved art is the ability to be both of the self and of the outside: a phenomenological condition, captured in the concept of intersubjectivity. This state enables corporeal engagement with one's environment as much as it does external observation and contextualization of the self in a field shaped not only by the individual, but also by others – including antagonists. Lassnig, then, displays a unique awareness of the nuances in observing, but, also, of being observed at the same time. That she interjects her self-image in its various iterations in her work renders the process of being observed doubly so: as the artist, whose work is looked at by others, but also as the subject of her own paintings, embedded within. This double sense of being scrutinized – by herself and by others, for the private person but no less for the professional persona, while being, precisely because of that very profession, deeply rooted within an artistic context, and the tensions this mounts, is captured in Crimp's protagonist, Julia, in *Men Asleep*.

Directed by Katie Mitchell, the premiere production of the play, a commission of the Deutsches Schauspielhaus Hamburg, opened in the spring of 2018.[1] The production made use of some of Mitchell's distinctive visual devices, also seen in her earlier work with Crimp: physical rewinding; stylized emphatic movement; the hypnotic slowing down of bodily activity, which, as one critic imagined, might have served as a device towards a reversal of the story – the pursuit of a different turn of events, which, however, as the reviewer continues, does not come to pass, because the zone of conflict [*Die Kampfzone*] persists (Laages 2018). Particularly in a play so invested in dialogue with visual art, such methods created the impression of an affective performative installation on a large-scale canvas. The cinemascope reminiscent field that Alex Eales's set brought to the MalerSaal (the more intimate space of the Schauspielhaus) accentuated this effect. As we do not have access to what transpires beyond the frames of the canvas, the dimensions and perimeter of Eales's set limited the parameters of vision, focusing the gaze but also disorientating us as to what remains tantalizingly, and, as I will go on to discuss, for the purposes of this production also strategically, out of view. The space towards the entrance of Julia and Paul's apartment, stage right, or the couple's bedroom, stage left, were visually off-limits for the audience. Characters, however, moved within those spaces, a fact that becomes highly meaningful when it comes to Mitchell's considerable intervention in the finale, which this chapter will also take into consideration.[2]

Agency, Actualization, Self-Affection

Men Asleep is a quietly multifaceted play, concerned with the ripple effects of desire, including its surge, sustenance, and expiration. It opens to Julia deep in conversation with her husband, Paul. She is delivering a lengthy monologue that appears to have been unfolding for a while. It touches on their long marriage, the lack of children, and Julia's conviction that they would not have made any kind of positive addition (91). A further point of emphasis is Julia's enduring commitment to the relationship:

> JULIA. [...W]e shan't divorce, Paul. Why should we divorce? [...] We split up and then what? And anyway, why? I don't suffer from my relationship with you. And you're not suffering – are you? – on account of me.
>
> (Crimp 2019d: 92)

In her torrential, yet composed and eloquent flow of words, the most startling part is not Julia's resolute dedication to the marriage, despite obvious dissatisfaction. It is not even the revelation that the issue of a child, indeed likely one that once almost existed (91), though, in Crimp's characteristic lack of disclosure it does not become clear that this was the case, or why it did not materialize, has come between the couple. The most startling admission is, rather, that the commitment to the relationship persists in spite of the fact that there is no desire in the couple.

This is, also, the singular point of information that receives the rawest exposition in Julia's monologue. We have heard the word 'desire' used previously in relation to a motherhood not pursued. Now sexual desire enters the conversational terrain, although a different term is used for it:

> JULIA. [...B]esides, since we've stopped loving each other, why would you test my love? [...] Oh you had a little fire once. And so did I. We both had a little more fire. Now we have none. Or next to none. Fire for our work perhaps.
>
> (91–92)

[...]

> You've lost interest in my mouth. You've lost interest in my eyes. You've lost interest in a lot of the things that interested you when you had more fire.
>
> (92)

In their study of desire and its performance in long-term marriages, sociologists Sinikka Elliott and Debra Umberson argue that 'Performing desire involves managing feelings around one's sexual relationship according to how one thinks desire should be both felt and performed, which is in turn linked to individuals' own and their spouse's expectations, beliefs, and experiences of gender, marriage, and heterosexuality' (2008: 394). Julia's opening monologue is loaded enough as it stands, but, when examined through such a lens, it reveals itself to be even more potent. Here, Julia inscribes her own narrative over the narrative of the marriage, co-authored by her and Paul, as a mode of vocalizing and owning not a sentimental disappointment, but the pragmatic state of affairs. As such, she also owns the text. There is indeed, also, a consideration of heterosexual attraction within a marriage – a precursor for events that follow, and which will confirm that heterosexual marriage, in the play, is revealed as a construct and a relic, at least in the case of Julia and Paul. The decline and absence of desire emerge strongly; we are confronted with these from the outset. In its negation as immaterial, desire emerges not only as affirmed, but, also, as dominant: the play's very plot pivot. It is desire for people, for command of their minds and/ or bodies; for success; for professional domination – and for the satisfaction, sometimes fleeting, others more enduring, that such attainment might bring.

Despite the late hour in which the plot is set, Julia is alert and far from sleep. In fact, as she notifies a stunned Paul, guests will soon be arriving. So they do: they are Josefine and Tilman, whose sudden presence sets up the scene for a confrontation between the middle-aged and the young couple. Julia and Paul are approaching fifty; Josefine is in her twenties and Tilman in his thirties. Like Julia, Josefine is an Art Historian, enthusiastically performing her gratitude for having secured a coveted position in Julia's academic department. Also like Julia, Josefine is, despite the time, wide-awake – even hyper. Tilman, the only non-academic in the group (he is a successful furniture company owner), on the contrary, seems confused, slow to react, out of his element. The same could be said of Paul, who, even though a, likewise, successful academic (his own domain is music), is not on a par with Julia in terms of intellectual or emotional rigour.

The play's electric intertextuality is responsive to Lassnig's sensibilities, as well as to Edward Albee's canonical tale of academics and their partners making their way deep into a night whose next day is uncertain: *Who's Afraid of Virginia Woolf* is, as Crimp highlights in his programme note (2018b), another point of departure (thus making the reference to a child, reminiscent of the most devastating revelation in

Albee's play, where the couple's son turns out to be fictional, yet more poignant). One reviewer identified even longer intertextual genealogies, pointing out Albee's own reliance upon August Strindberg's *The Dance of Death* [*Dödsdansen*, 1900] in terms of the depiction of conflict between woman and man (Laages 2018). In *Men Asleep*, however, unlike the representations of female characters in Albee's play as either bitter and substance-dependent or largely frivolous and inconsequential, and of academia as a gendered trope and form of gentlemen's agreement, we are dealing with a kind of academic female legacy – what, to borrow from Sandra M. Gilbert, we might describe as a dynamic representation of the function of 'powerful literary ancestresses' (Gilbert 1985: 355). Here, this is conceptualized as an initiation to the academic ritual and preparation for eventual bequeathing of the authority and responsibility, but, also, the tough choices that come with it, from Julia to Josefine. Gilbert's term implies a textual continuity; the formation of a tradition where texts speak to one another: what Gilbert and Susan Gubar, in their earlier joint seminal work *The Madwoman in the Attic* (1979) identify as a 'literary sub-culture, a community in which women consciously read and related to each other's works', which, in the time elapsed since the authors' nineteenth-century paradigms, or even in the decades since their book first appeared, seems to have systematically exposed and counteracted 'male literary assertion and coercion' (Gilbert and Gubar 2020: xii). In the context of everything being a narrative, Julia's career and her formidable success is also one; her professional path-crossing with Josefine invites the latter to intersect with her senior colleague's narrative and superscribe her own take on female academia, through her own perspective and agency.

Still, nothing is straightforward in such careers, and nothing in Crimp's play is reductive in its representation of them, either; likewise, no assumptions can be easily made as to the countermanding of control mechanisms, especially when these are performed as subtly and effectively as we encounter here: through male partners that are passive on the surface, and proven aggressive when the play begins to peel the more intimate layers of the relationships concerned. A layering of personal and professional narratives, then, to match the complexity of the issues the play takes on. As Gilbert and Gubar rightly recognize in their more recent joint publication, *Still Mad: American Women Writers and the Feminist Imagination 1950–2020* (2021), which offers an assessment of the past seventy years in women's literary-social activity in the United States, and in the face of rapidly shifting ground, the process of self-assertion and counteraction is ongoing. In the opening section of their book ('Introduction: The Possible and the Impossible'), Gilbert and Gubar rightly identify the election of Donald J. Trump (2016) as a watershed moment for the displacement by men running on bravado as experienced by highly qualified women. *Men Asleep* appears, crucially, in 2018, with two highly articulate, talented, and different women as focal points of the plot. I am drawn here to the assessment that Gilbert and Gubar offer, and which, in my view, the play heeds: 'that we are entering an era when it will be more important than ever to examine women's lives, dreams, hopes, and despairs' (2021: 13) as a mode of 'counter[ing] the shocking legitimization of misogyny in our time' (2021: 18).

This misogyny takes many forms, and the importance of *Men Asleep* is that it highlights some of the darker, however insipid ones, from institutional suppression to spousal sabotage. Not all forms of misogyny are equally obvious, but they are all equally catastrophic, the play shows us. I am also especially struck by the framing that Gilbert and Gubar offer as to the selection of their case studies in *Still Mad*: 'We were drawn not only to the publications of notable women but also to their lives, which dramatize the problems flesh-and-blood women face as they make the personal political', they note (2). The publications and accolades of women – their intellectual and physical output – are essential to bring to light, and Julia and Josefine's qualifications are discussed often; the play pursues this resolutely. At the same time, it also delivers the fleshiness that reveals women's lives in the way they are experienced in the domain that informs, but that also exists as discreet from the work: the domestic, the quotidian, the intimate. Here, then, lies Crimp's interventionist intertextuality: speaking to a play (*Who's Afraid of Virginia Woolf*), itself an intertext given its title reference, no less, which, arguably, conceptualizes women as less than agents in any fruitful way, and to a painting (*Schlafende Männer*) where the absence of women is as disquieting as the utter abandon of men, implying a degree of quiet, yet effective and deeply problematic privileged agency, Crimp addresses what it is, in the decades since the earlier play – broadly the period that Gilbert and Gubar themselves are concerned with – that has landed women at the forefront of the public realm, but has, at the same time, denied them the kind of equality that might render them indeed free from oppression. This is the kind of equality that would also render women non-vilified on the basis of the choices they have made relating to their bodies; or, similarly, unimpeded by the institutional structures that have proclaimed to become more welcoming, more elastic, more equitable, all the while oppressing – except in more subtle modes of coercion. The effort to claim space for and by women, as Gilbert and Gubar argue, and as *Men Asleep* depicts, remains 'tremulous, tumultuous, tremendous, ongoing' (2021: 2). The play is as much concerned with the legacies of the artistic canon as with the legacies existing between individuals – but narratives are never fixed, and storylines are there to be disrupted, as we come to be reminded over the course of performance.

The concept of 'self-affection', which Luce Irigaray develops with specific reference to the work of Lassnig, captures sensuous, mental, and emotional states that speak to the corporeality of Crimp's *Men Asleep*, especially given the intertextual links between the two works. Judith Still's analysis of self-affection in Irigaray is also of value, not least because the broader narrative within which it materializes concerns ideas of hospitality: the very context that gives rise to the events of *Men Asleep*. As Still argues, via Irigaray, hospitality and self-affection are formative experiences: a question of opening up one's world to the stranger, while, as the same time, preserving one's own sense of self (2012: 41). Irigaray, as Still notes, 'insists […] that we should be faithful to our own manner of dwelling – and yet be willing to be changed by encounter', since 'a true welcome, for Irigaray, implies the possibility of constructing a new and third world as a result of my world's meeting with that of the other' (2012: 41). Within this context, there must be a flow that enables self-affection: 'For the subject to experience himself, or herself, as both affecting and affected, an inward space must be created in which the two take place thanks to a temporal delay in which the active relates to the passive', writes Irigaray (Still 2012: 42).

Defining 'self-affection' is not straightforward, though Irigaray's paradigm of the middle-passive voice provides grounding: in Greek, the middle-passive is the linguistic framing of an act that means that I, as subject, both produce the activity *and* am impacted by it, as an object would be – therefore the active and the passive meet in one and the same moment, and/or event (Still 2012: 42). In *Men Asleep*, Mitchell's techniques produced a temporal elasticity that rendered self-affection evident. Though all characters experience such moments of intimate reckoning, ultimately it is Julia's self-affection that both text and production foreground. It is helpful, further, to consider Irigaray's description of self-affection as:

> a process which takes place before any particular perception of the self, any sensitive or mental conscious experience. A process which has not yet really been taken into consideration although it determines our feelings and thoughts without being ever expressed as such. It remains a sort of invisible and silent framework which is able to gather together our whole being. […T]o perceive this

process of self-affection requires a real autonomy, a faithfulness to our self and a capacity of concentrating but also of letting be, of letting exist or live.

(2006: 66–67)

Irigaray emphasizes the profundity of the individual unto herself and, at the same time, as agent in a process of connection and interaction with her environment that will shape *her* as much as *it*, and that is both the state of existing (present stage) and the direct outcome of her positioning and experience (next stage). The latter is also contingent on the visitor – the external agent. As Still notes, we must anticipate 'that the encounter with the other is not necessarily cosy or comfortable' given that 'The other interrupts the system of cross-references of my world, re-opens my horizon and questions its finality. As such the other undoes the familiarity that was mine' (2012: 50).

As we have seen, *Men Asleep* opens with an exposition of Julia and Paul's cross-referentiality as a couple; theirs is a tight, intricately woven system of communication and private codes, honed through years of familiarity. The wear-and-tear keeps resurfacing in dialogue, especially as the couples are getting to know each other: Julia and Paul's is not a comfortable, or cosy marriage, unlike Josefine's persistent references to their so-perceived normality. Moreover, the couple's inter-dependence is tangible. Their inner thread becomes disrupted as a result of that 'encounter with the other' and as the night unfolds, with boundaries of propriety dissolving and the visit delivering a decisive fissure in the characters' lives; an act, perhaps, that Julia desires so as to perturb the stilted personal context. Crimp's play develops self-affection as both the act of being and becoming at the same time, a formative gesture that is primarily self-directed in the case of each individual character, though its consequences will also impact others. The night is a vehicle of re-discovery of the self, and, by means of that, also of transformation.

I find Irigaray's assertion that 'If a masculine picture generally seems to be a little frozen, a feminine picture rather looks moving' (2006: 37) particularly relevant to the present discussion. In his reflection on *Schlafende Männer* [the Lassnig painting], Crimp weighs the absence of women, contemplating the apparent relaxed stillness of the men: 'And what has happened to the women, exactly?', he asks ['Und was genau ist mit den Frauen passiert?'] (2018b). The approach that Crimp takes to the depiction of male stillness – metaphorically, in terms of being emotionally, and, to an extent, mentally stunted, but also literally, as in the state of sleep, a physical and emotional self-withdrawal – exposes the difference between male and female engagement with self and

environment. The text absorbs the absence of women in Lassnig's specific painting and thematically extends it, thereby being receptive of
the broader context of Lassnig's work and its strong feminist element,
to indict the systemic patriarchal structures that process women's confidence and ambition as aggression. Having emphasized the inequalities
in the exertion of women and men in the workplace by pinpointing
Paul and Tilman's success despite their evidently lacklustre personalities
and juxtaposing this with Julia and Josefine's fiery dedication to their
respective work, the text proceeds to demonstrate how the systematic
erasure of women from narratives of professional power has in fact produced a reactionary act of solidarity and strength. It is important that,
in the finale, whether in the text or in the premiere production, we
see only the women; it is now the absence of men that is conspicuous.
Irigaray notes: 'A man needs some effort to set the shapes in motion
while, for a woman, they are constantly one way or another on the
move' (2006: 37). Indefatigable, the women go on working into the
night; the men are no longer part of the play's canvas. Julia's narrative
of self-affection – of both driving the action and absorbing its consequences – serves to focus the gaze; it is Julia's point of view that
undoubtedly emerges as dominant.

Desire and/as Disturbance

Through the commanding presence of Julia Wieninger, the Hamburg
production established Julia as the lead early on – in control so absolutely, that when her inner confidence is threatened this becomes doubly disconcerting. In *The Rest Will Be Familiar to You from Cinema (Alles
Weitere kennen Sie aus dem Kino)*, in whose premiere Wieninger played
Iokaste (Jocasta in the English playtext), as in *Men Asleep*, the female
lead once more emerged as dominant, her voice and comportment
exuding strength even in moments of radical uncertainty. Intertextual
and inter-production connections continued with Paul Herwig, who,
embodying Paul in *Men Asleep*, had also previously played Kreon in
the premiere of *The Rest Will Be Familiar to You from Cinema*. This
is a character that felt compelled to overperform his masculinity in
order to assert his political authority without, at the same time, being
able to command the respect, or reach the inner certitude, that his
sister Iokaste had already accomplished. We are, moreover, in both
cases, dealing with two female protagonists in problematic marriages,
who are, however, formidable managers of the situations surrounding them at times of crisis, and who emerge as strong examples for
younger women, rising above the feebleness of men and the blockages

this creates. Julia is not Josefine's mother, as Iokaste is to Antigone in the earlier play (discussed in detail further on), but she is the one who enables the beginning of Josefine's professional path, which is a form of professional mothering.

Reflecting on the stillness in the body postures of the five men depicted in Lassnig's *Schlafende Männer*, lying on a surface that looks like concrete but is difficult to distinguish precisely, perhaps relaxing, perhaps, even, on holiday, Crimp makes an observation: despite the title, one man is reading – clearly not sleeping (Crimp 2018b). We might say that Lassnig's male figures, like Crimp's, may not necessarily be literally sleeping, but are, as far as empathy is concerned, rather anaesthetized. The dynamics in dialogue between Julia and Josefine are sharp and focused. It is not so with the men, who are given, in both plays, to sudden outbursts and vulnerabilities, evident also in their soft and nervous speech tones. When it comes to Paul, this is a manifestation of his humdrum personality and overall mediocrity; in the case of Tilman, we are effectively dealing with jejune concentration deficit. Such is the broader corporeal field on which the crisis of masculinity that both men experience is built. What both Lassnig's painting and Crimp's play capture is that men, whether singularly or in their social circles, have the capacity to become detached – especially so from the emotional worlds of women. That there is no female presence in Lassnig's painting is telling: the simplicity and abandon in the men's poses allow no space for her; they have taken up the space for themselves, excluding her resolutely.

Themes of passive-aggressive patriarchy emerge in the play with regularity, as art and life, and art *in* life, merge in ways dangerous and unpredictable. For example, as a response to Julia's opening monologue, selectively quoted above, Paul proceeds with his own, where he makes sure to deploy her devotion to work as a means of undermining her. This allows us to gauge, in the process, Paul's own feelings of inadequacy at the fact that he could never match the desire for devotion that Julia has exhibited towards her work:

PAUL. Even at weekends you went into your department and worked. You worked through bombings. You worked through murder. Not one murder stopped you working – right through the night if necessary.

(93)

Later on, Paul directs the following comment towards Josefine, a snide remark disguised as compliment:

PAUL. You remind me of Ulrike Meinhof.
[…]
PAUL. Don't you think? – don't you think? – something about that
    smile.
JOSEFINE. Ulrike Meinhof killed herself.

(95)

It is not irrelevant that Paul makes this statement immediately after
Josefine's somewhat absurdist oversharing concerning her very active
(and sometimes drug-fuelled) sex life with Tilman, which she uses to
deliver an underhanded compliment to Julia and Paul, who are 'both so
stable' (95), in a very long relationship, as she emphasizes, and, therefore,
the complete opposite of her and Tilman. That Paul undercuts desire
with death through the Meinhof reference is, of course, not an acci-
dent – he is looking to unsettle and disorientate Josefine. Nonetheless,
however momentarily thrown, Josefine will not appear defeated. That
Paul's passive-aggressiveness is a symptom of his need for constant vali-
dation will emerge at different points in the play, from seemingly casual
remarks to his outright sexual overture towards Tilman. His antago-
nism against Josefine, therefore, is not merely an expression of his jealousy because she has earned Julia's (professional) respect and attention,
which he has not, necessarily, attained himself; it is also a manifestation
of his lack as a lover, in the face of being confronted with a couple
whose life is brimming with expressed, mutual desire.

Another example of the reach and depth of patriarchal dominance
and its inflexible strategies, which force more amenable subjects to
become doubly flexible so as to prevent the breakdown of productivity
(mental and material) comes with reference to the professional domain
and how its demands infringe upon personal space (again both mental
and material). *Men Asleep* features a device reminiscent of *The Country*:
an oppressive, absent male character rendered present by means of his
phone call. In the earlier play, this is Morris, a doctor and colleague
of Richard's, calling to assert his authority and apply pressure on an
already difficult situation, where Richard has failed to uphold professional standards. His constant presence is particularly oppressive to
Corinne, who perceives him as an overall source of interference and
control over the couple's lives. In *Men Asleep*, the character is Marko, an
artist, Julia's professional acquaintance. On the occasion of an exhibition
opening, he calls from Los Angeles to ask Julia to write the catalogue
text, adapting her work from an earlier project. In order to be acceptable to Marko, the updated version must omit any contextual reference
to other artists so as to showcase his work. When Julia exclaims that

through such an omission her argument will be jeopardized, Marko is unreserved in performing the inflexibility of his demand, becoming aggressive. Julia is irritated, but the professional opportunity for public exposure is considerable. It is this pragmatism that she will pass on to Josefine when, by break of day, she will ask her to make the changes to the text as Marko requested them. When Josefine queries this, Julia is resolute: this level of adaptability is essential to sustain her kind of successful career, she says (140). We may choose to view this as compromise; or we may choose to interpret it as lucid pragmatism and as a form of serving oneself and one's own ambition; the latter is, after all, a desire that, for Julia, no other state of being has ever been able to match.

Certainly it is not the marriage that will ever displace the allure of professional acclaim from its prime position: everything about Julia and Paul's marriage is – and apparently always has been – tepid. Even the way in which Josefine talks about water, a recurring theme in the play, particularly around the fact that in Julia and Paul's apartment drinking water only ever seems to come in a lukewarm temperature and always needs to run to become borderline drinkable, is a metaphor for the state of a relationship. The tone in which Josefine addresses the issue not only reveals this fact about Julia and Paul's marriage, but also Josefine's readiness to address sex and desire – which stems from her own confidence in such matters:

JOSEFINE. I think what the water's thinking about is its journey through the human body. It's going to be inside you like a lover is. So it sits there in the pipe waiting and wondering who it's going to penetrate.

(101)

Sexual imagery continues to be charged throughout, sometimes verbally, and sometimes physically. Instances include: when the men find themselves briefly alone, Paul asks Tilman what his reaction would be if he [Paul] were to ask him [Tilman] to kiss him, which Tilman rebuffs (104); when the running joke of whether Josefine and Paul ought to have a boxing fight escalates and she actually punches Paul, Tilman '*Very gently* [...] *starts to wipe away the blood from Paul's face*' (110); Josefine and Tilman's protracted kiss, witnessed by Julia and Paul (111); Tilman's request to Josefine to inquire after Paul's professional activity – strangely late into the night, immediately following the kiss, and likely an expression of flirtation directed from Tilman to Paul. The latter also prompts Julia to inform the guests that Paul 'makes dance music' (112) and to elaborate:

JULIA. [...] And it's perfectly true that he himself doesn't dance – any more than I do – not in that way – [...]. But why not trust it if it gives you pleasure? Because I'm all for pleasure – I've nothing against pleasure – I simply don't experience it anymore.

[...]

TILMAN. But you must get pleasure from writing a book.

JULIA. Pleasure? (112)

Desire and pleasure, then, are distinct; one does not necessarily imply the other for Julia, because it is not a human agent that procures the former; it is work. At the same time, Julia is entirely prepared to address the facile generalization of the term 'pleasure', querying its applicability to labour – however dedicated she may be to it, and however, equally, driven by it. There are further instances: in assessing her own agency, especially as a mentor to female colleagues, Julia makes a reference that extends beyond the realm of the working environment:

JULIA. [...] I mean I try and take care of the young women in my department but once they've left the building they are totally in the hands of others and what happens to them in the hands of others is none of my business – they can dance till the daylight comes – they can fuck till they're bruised inside – and if men want to take them home, if men want to wrap them up in bed, with just their heads poking out, I can understand that. Because I think I am right in saying that we women can go on, we can go on and on and on. Whereas men like to sleep. Is that not so, Tilman?

(114–115)

And while on a basic interpretative level Julia's comments might be classed as prurient, the meaning, here, is deeper than that. Julia's reference remains in the broader context of her primary discourse thread: women are natural workers, men are not; women are resilient, men are meek; men may perform care as a means of control, but it is women who are making the choices – of labour, of sexuality, of self-disposal, of partnership; including any compromise that the latter might entail.

Earlier on, we have also heard Josefine express this – she takes care of the body through exercise, she says, but it is the library that primarily occupies her time (110); another rigorous form of discipline, and no less demanding. There are two forces engaged in the territorial claim of Josefine's mental and physical capacity here: one is research; the other is marriage. Julia has, after all, assigned Josefine the task of writing on the Renaissance, considerably outside of her primary expertise, a labour that Julia may see as a form of care, of protection from her perceived banality of the private realm (110). Tilman, on the other hand, is the father of Josefine's unborn child, and is, therefore, perceiving the primacy in that aspect of their lives. Now it is Josefine who must negotiate her professional and personal selves; but when it comes to Julia, there is no ambiguity as to which takes precedence. Rather than make this appear the outcome of a resignation from one's inner emotional and/or sexual life, the play offers us the above statement by Julia to underline that, as a heterosexual woman, where the weighing factor rests for her in assigning primacy to the professional domain is the inadequacy of men. This includes their self-casting in the role of protector as a form of asserting power, because they are aware that they could not be, in any other meaningful sense, an equal partner. The two sides of her life that Josefine must negotiate are delineated further when Tilman accuses Julia of making Josefine drink when the two women momentarily step away from the apartment (unseen by the audience); Julia corrects him that it was Josefine, in fact, who requested that they have a drink (123). To make the point yet more emphatically, Julia dismisses the '[...] fuss about alcohol – all this concern about coffee' (123) as 'just new forms of control – [...] And whenever a woman escapes one form of control, another is immediately invented' (124). For Julia, calculated tenderness is another of these forms of cruelty and control; a counterforce to women's propensity for being productive, for being creative; another sanctioned form of jurisdiction over women's bodies.

Therefore, when Josefine enters a long monologue, all the while managing Tilman's physical performance of his lust towards her, which now crosses over to the socially inappropriate (he begins to unbutton her trousers), and is still able to assert the following, this is quite meaningful:

JOSEFINE. [...] I don't need to be told that I smile like Ulrike Meinhof, you [Paul] don't need to make me think about ideology and death, I think every day about ideology and death – Julia too, we can't help it, we like it – ideology and death – it's our domain.

(127)

Within the context of the characters' conversation, Meinhof also functions intertextually (the effect is, therefore double) within a narrative of youth, aggression and ultimate defeat/failure, or resignation, that Paul is attempting to superscribe on Josefine. Josefine, however, is highly confident and skilled at seeing herself objectively – for her talent, her strengths, her potential – as Julia can also do very well for both herself and Josefine. Consequently, neither woman is ultimately susceptible, or indeed vulnerable, to Paul's reductive attacks, or even his targeted, seemingly arbitrary categorization; to his attempts at classifying someone as a type and inscribing precariousness on her. Josefine, here, seems to be reinforcing Julia's point (made, especially, when Tilman discusses 'pleasure' in the context of finishing a book; to Julia, the concept does not apply in that context): women are able to be multitask, men are not; women are able to distinguish between the domains of life – men are not; which is why, ultimately, men are equally likely to appear listless in either the personal, or the professional, or both. Women craft themselves, including as workers, with discipline, poise, and commitment. Such is the range of reference of the play – and men cannot necessarily match this, or they choose not to, imposing often toxic, objectifying narratives of categorizations on women. In Crimp's plays, and very much in the specific one, women are agents – they are self-actualizers, and they remain attuned to their environment, and to others. It is an intersubjectivity that, the play suggests, men are not necessarily capable of, or, at least, not equally invested in.

It is some way into the play, likely sensing that his connection to Tilman is evolving, that Paul makes a reference to the beginnings of his relationship with Julia and how physical this was in their youth (120). Similarly, perhaps sensing the transition in Tilman, Josefine repeatedly requests that he affirm his love for her (124, 126), while, at the same time, emphasizing that her own attachment to Tilman is not primarily intellectual, but erotic (126). For his part, and performing, more than any other character, the play's dialogue with its Absurdist intertextual reference, Tilman appears increasingly unable to restrain his sexual urges, becoming physical with Josefine. At one point, as mentioned earlier, he begins to unbutton her trousers while she speaks (126), an act that, considered alongside his suggestion to Paul, moments earlier, that they might visit his music studio, reveals a burgeoning desire that is now beginning to unravel. It is not out of context then, that a perceptive Josefine remarks on how, uncommonly for her, she does not seem to be attracting Paul's sexual interest (127). Earlier on, as part of her now established antagonistic banter with Paul, she suggests that he might 'get [...Tilman] to dance to your dance music' (126). Paul retorts that he will (127). Tilman's sexuality, other than a point of latent negotiation between two desirous parties – Josefine and Paul – also becomes a subject for Julia quite overtly not long after, when she uses a seemingly passing reference to material possessions as a way of asking Tilman whether he 'collects women' or 'maybe he collects men' (130).

The stage of escalation arrives when Tilman feels that Josefine is slipping away from his grasp now that her career is beginning in earnest. First, he comments on a change in the colour of her eyes (135); then he hears Julia intercept Josefine's instinctive response that she will now take Tilman home – to a context of intimacy we have previously heard about, one that would place desire for the body over desire for labour, one that would also, of course, limit Julia's involvement – and undercut it by stressing that it was her expectation that she and Josefine would go on to work, rather than sleep (136). It is then that he suddenly asks:

TILMAN. But Paul have you ever hit / *a man*?

To which comes the reply:

PAUL. Of course I've hit a man. I hit men / all the time.

(136)

The point of Paul not hitting women, whether it be Julia, or Josefine, has been made earlier. For Josefine, it is in the context of their play-fighting, that indeed lands Paul with an injury. Tilman's words – 'Hit me now then' (136), repeated, are an invitation to an act different from that which they suggest, which is not, by any means, an attempt towards a glorification of sexual violence. This is also proven by the stage direction, which makes it clear that there is no form of violence between the two men, but, rather, a continuation of Tilman's comment from mere moments before that 'Dr Haas [Paul] made me a proposition earlier' (125). As the segment closes, preparing us for the final scene, we have reached the climax of Crimp's quietly explosive text. While Tilman invites Paul to hit him, Crimp's text reads:

Tilman has completed his journey towards Paul, and now puts his arms around
    him as if he needs Paul's support to keep standing.
[…]
The two men sway together. […]

(137)

On the basis of the text, as well as the premiere production, spectators will not see the two men in the final scene, which concentrates on Julia in work mode, as Josefine enters the living room. It is implied that perhaps she has been sleeping, especially as she is uncertain as to the whereabouts of Paul and Tilman.

It was at this point that Mitchell's staging added a considerable super-script to Crimp's text. The way in which events unfold in the play itself reveals nothing as to what transpired since we last saw the two men.

Josefine is tired; she remarks on the sunrise and attempts to establish whether – and when – Tilman and Paul returned from the visit to Paul's studio. Julia informs Josefine that her husband is sleeping (141) and that she closed the door to the room (142), presumably so as not to disturb. According to the text, in the beginning of the scene, before Josefine enters, Julia is shown to us as distracted – exhibiting signs not only of mental, but also of physical discomfort, as she experiences a gag reflex, which she resolutely brings under control (138). 'Discipline' in all its iterations is key here: the descriptor stands for both the concept of academic domain, as well as for the process of applying oneself fully. As such, it is the ultimate determiner of Julia's identity: the body performs it wholly. This is not shown as a negative – not as a qualifier of women's hardening, or lack of empathy; it is shown as a matter of fact. Desire, if it is to be felt, lies in the moments of self-affirmation: it is a desire for the true self, and so it is self-experienced, and self-directed. For others in the play, however, desire is externalized.

The suggestion of a burgeoning desire between Paul and Tilman might mean that they never returned from the studio, where they spent the night together; that indeed they returned, and spent the night together in the couple's apartment; or any other similar deduction. In Crimp's text, the insinuation that Julia has committed any kind of violent act against the two men is never made as such. This was, however, the interpretation that Mitchell's production pursued, as in the opening of the final scene we see Julia emerging from the direction of the bedroom holding a bloodied knife, presumably having attacked the two men, who, in the scene transition prior to the finale were shown as walking in slow motion towards the bedroom. Of course, the text does not rule out any version of events categorically, either. As in *The Country* the fate of one character (Rebecca) quietly remains a mystery at the end of the play, so, here, ambiguity lingers over both the status of Tilman and Paul's relationship and their current whereabouts. While recognizing that such statements are, to an extent, subjective and motivated by one's own spectatorial sensibility, but also being mindful of the overall tone of Crimp's playwriting – which steers clear of 'telling' – I wonder whether the considerably unambiguous visual statement of what has transpired in the gap might in fact have been a rather heavy load to land on the play. Crimp's text is potent in its rising tension and restrained escalation; there is no moment of spectacular discovery. To suggest that there is, in my view, might detract from the potency of conjecture and the density of emotion, which, otherwise, Crimp's piece builds up affectively.

Julia begins the play by expressing her incredulity that there may be space left for an impassioned gesture – like a kiss, specifically – between her and Paul. So she embarks, in the presence of others, whom she admits as agents, and, still, solitary, through the night, on an act of self-assertion, open to being tested through the encounter – and, more importantly, the confrontation with – the Other. Julia has braced herself for the journey, knowing that the ultimate base for her lies within: her home is herself, and her work. Irigaray writes:

> [...] it can be understood that after flowing outside herself, mingling with the environment, a woman wants to return home, within herself. Maria Lassnig thus wonders about the limits between the surroundings and herself. One could say that she is in search of a skin. [...] It is true that the skin is also porous and does not secure a real envelope with regard to the surroundings. Also through the skin it is possible that some confusion exists between the inside and the outside. A mixing that self-affecting could avoid or enjoy [...].
> (44–45)

In the textual version of the finale, Julia has returned home. The visceral struggle is shown to us as self-affecting in Julia's moment of nausea, and her perseverance: she is absorbing and adapting to a new reality. The body exhibits the signs, responding to the triggers of the mind – and she disciplines herself, reconnecting to her core. The work continues.

As Crimp shows us in *Men Asleep*, and as he has previously shown, especially in *The Country*, the most transgressive acts between couples are often carried out without express violence. The abuse (mental and emotional rather than physical), rather, is chronic; it is latent. It is transactional pragmatism, not love, and certainly not desire that primarily preserves marriages. The violence, therefore, does not require an act of climax – its very power emerges from the fact that it is a dense presence, pervasive, unresolved. It is the act of standing successfully on a tightrope, and negotiating the sense of self and identity – the wild inner life that emerges from these – alongside the decay of an insidious, corrosive relationship that is the primary challenge. The sacrifice is enough, and it does not mandate further dramatic escalation; the crisis and the crime are no less real without it.

Closing Reflections

Through its field of action, as well as its intertextual references, *Men Asleep* emerges as play invested in exploring desire; it delves in what it is that brings the latter to existence; specifically, whether it is a drive to succeed professionally, or to possess a partner that is the most dominant urge. Another concern of the play is the viability of desire – its tena-bility and repercussions; its projections onto others, as well as on the self – in a sense of fulfilment stemming from within, self-directed and self-affected. Despite the social composition of the group in terms of professions and achievement, no ground is ceded to the cerebral over the corporeal, in the sense that both are equally acknowledged for their significance and no superiority is claimed for either. Lust, or embodied desire, emerges as a force equally dominant to intellectual curiosity. In Mitchell's production, of course, the play also took on the addi-tional layer of death *and* desire, which this book goes on to examine specifically in its final chapter. Desire and death are shown to be in a relationship of mutual implication, and, even though spectators could not be sure as to the precise transgression that Julia has committed, it is implied that it was – at the very least – considerable, if not fatal. The intertextual connection to Lassnig's painting is, perhaps, the most tell-ing one: quiet anticipation, or, perhaps, resignation, burgeoning with an action that is latent, disturbing a field of quiet, pregnant with erup-tion, the moment that Lassnig captures is anything other than calm. Such is Crimp's play, too. In the finale of the text as published, perhaps Paul and Tilman are, indeed, literally asleep – but perhaps they are not. Surely, however, they have been shown to be emotionally and empath-ically so throughout the play.

Contextualizing their choice of title in *Still Mad*, Gilbert and Gubar write: 'Mad as in the sense of enraged. Mad as in the sense of mad-dened, confused, or rebellious' (3). And, then, more powerfully still, in their own intertextual engagement with viral slogans that have penetrated the cultural realm: 'Maybe if you come a long way, you encounter territorial backlash. Maybe if you shatter glass ceilings, you have to walk on broken glass. Maybe if you lean in, you topple over' (3). The risks for women are emotional, mental, physical – there is no such thing as a safe zone, no gain without compromise. But it is presence, perhaps, that is the ultimate in perseverance; presence and endurance. In its nods to other texts, once more, both verbal and visual, *Men Asleep* is playful, but it also builds – and sustains – a quiet darkness and tentativeness that are very much Crimp's own. Once the eruption has happened, strengths of will are tested; and, indeed, so is the greatest desire of them all, the one for self-preservation, personal and professional. Resilience emerges as its natural partner. The men that occupy Lassnig's frame have disappeared in Crimp's. Julia is as towering a figure as Martha in Albee's *Who's Afraid of Virginia Woolf*, but wholly sober – no amount of external control can curb her drive, and this is, ultimately, the lesson she will impart on her new colleague.

The dawn arrives, eventually. The women, as Julia predicted, have endured. And, so, Julia and Josefine emerge on the other side of the *Walpurgisnacht* to write another page.

Notes

1. All references to the performance refer to my experience of the live show on 26 March 2018.
2. For a recent discussion of Katie Mitchell's approach to Martin Crimp's work from an angle focused on the director, see: Fowler, B. (2021) *Katie Mitchell: Beautiful Illogical Acts*. London and New York: Routledge.

Bibliography

Albee, E. (2001) *Who's Afraid of Virginia Woolf?* London: Vintage Books.

Crimp, M. (2000a) *The Country*. London: Faber & Faber.

Crimp, M. (2018b) Programme Note, in *Schlafende Männer Theatre Programme*. Hamburg: Deutsches Schauspielhaus Hamburg.

Crimp, M. (2019d) *Men Asleep*, in Crimp, M. *The Hamburg Plays*. London: Faber & Faber, pp. 85–146.

Elliott, S. and Umberson, D. (2008) 'The Performance of Desire: Gender and Sexual Negotiation in Long-Term Marriages', *Journal of Marriage and Family*, 70(4), pp. 391–406.

Gilbert, S. M. (1985) 'Life's Empty Pack: Notes Toward a Literary Daughteronomy', *Critical Inquiry*, 11(3), pp. 355–384.

Gilbert, S. M. and Gubar, S. (2020) *The Madwoman in the Attic: The Woman Writer and the Nineteenth-Century Literary Imagination*. New Haven and London: Yale University Press.

Gilbert, S. M. and Gubar, S. (2021) *Still Mad: American Women Writers and the Feminist Imagination 1950–2020*. New York: W. W. Norton.

Irigaray, L. (2006) 'Wie lässt sich weibliche Selbst-Affektion zum Erscheinen bringen?/How to Make Feminine Self-Affection Appear?', in Pakesch, P. (ed.), Exhibition Catalogue for *Zwei oder Drei oder Etwas/Two or Three or Something*, Kunsthaus Graz am Landesmuseum Joanneum, 4 February–7 May. Available at: https://www.museum-joanneum.at/fileadmin/user_upload/Presse/Aktuelle_Projekte/Archiv/2006/zwei-oder-drei-oder-/Katalog_Zwei_20oder_20Drei_1_.pdf (Accessed 23 Dec. 2021).

Laages, M. (2018) 'Kein Frieden im Krieg der Geschlechter'. Available at: https://www.deutschlandfunkkultur.de/schlafende-maenner-in-hamburg-kein-frieden-im-krieg-der-100.html (Accessed: 21 Dec. 2021).

Lassnig, M. (2006) *Schlafende Männer*. [Oil on canvas.] Available at: https://arts-sceniques.be/rencontre/des-hommes-endormis/ (Accessed: 21 Dec. 2021).

Still, J. (2012) 'Sharing the World: Luce Irigaray and the Hospitality of Difference', *L'Esprit Créateur*, 52(3), pp. 40–51.

Strindberg, A. (2021) *Dödsdansen*. Copenhagen: Saga Egmont.

3 Handling with Care

Cyrano de Bergerac and *When We Have Sufficiently Tortured Each Other*

If the past decade has been a very fruitful period for Martin Crimp overall, then 2018 and 2019 stand out as particularly exceptional years: 2018 saw the premieres of *Men Asleep* and *Lessons in Love and Violence*; 2019 began with *When We Have Sufficiently Tortured Each Other* (subtitle: *Twelve Variations on Samuel Richardson's Pamela*) and closed with *Cyrano de Bergerac*. The former opened at the Dorfman auditorium of the National Theatre in January;[1] the latter at the Playhouse Theatre in November (both London).[2] Both productions featured highly prominent actors in lead roles: Cate Blanchett and James McAvoy respectively. *Cyrano de Bergerac* was a West End show drawing in considerable crowds, leading to a sell-out run; the same was the case with *When We Have Sufficiently Tortured Each Other*, for which the National Theatre implemented an unusual for the venue ballot ticketing policy as a strategy for managing the demand. Both texts produce radical responses to the source material, dealing with the darker, more ravaging aspects of desire. The specific approach to intertextuality that Crimp adopts in these projects, of course, plays a major role in my decision to combine them within a framework of analysis. It is, however, the intrigue of desire that serves as the primary point of interconnection – a desire exposed for what it is in its primal formats: never temperate; never noble; always selfish, and always uncontainable.

That two older, canonical texts serve as vehicles for astute representations of modern love and sexuality in all their iterations without the result coming across as in any way dated, but, on the contrary, entirely attuned to its context and sharply contemporary is a testament to Crimp's ear for language. This result is also, as I have discussed elsewhere (Angelaki 2012: 153–176), a product of Crimp's ability to mediate effectively between different cultural and linguistic communities, as well as between different spatial and social contexts. Both source texts date back centuries: Richardson's to the mid-eighteenth (1740–41)

DOI: 10.4324/9781003033400-4

and Rostand's to the late nineteenth (1897). Crimp's extensive activity in translation and adaptation – without seeking to conflate the two, but, rather, looking to capture Crimp's engagement with the literary canon – is well documented: projects have included reworkings of texts reaching as far back as the ancient Greek tragedians (as this volume also discusses) and as close to the present as contemporary European playwrights, with considerable attention paid to the French canon, into which Crimp has delved consistently, especially as a translator.

This chapter does not aim to discuss either *Cyrano de Bergerac* (Crimp's reworking) or *When We Have Sufficiently Tortured Each Other* by placing them in direct comparison with the source texts that have inspired them. Rather, while appreciating the literary context and, to a certain extent, the relationships of these pieces to their antecedents, the approach I will be taking will link these plays to my remaining case studies by means of a specific, shared thematic focus. While intertextuality is a significant consideration, understanding how Crimp highlights the most intimate and fraught aspects of interpersonal relationships, dealing with eroticisms dark and dangerous, serves as the main unifying thread for this discussion, not least in terms of variation and exchange in what, proceeding from Pierre Bourdieu, has been described as '*erotic capital* and its relationship to sexual stratification' (Green 2011: 245; emphasis original). In the context of this chapter, 'erotic capital' denotes the authority a lover brings, and the power they can wield. All the while, language is fierce and second to none other element in these texts: its embodied, voluminous twists and turns give physical desire a direct match and contender. If longing is an all-consuming state, in these texts this is manifest fully, as all individual processes are dedicated to the same cause: conquest.

In an effusive review of *Cyrano* for *The New York Times*, one critic emphasizes the romance of, and for language, as a dominant characteristic of the play that emerges from the early moments, aptly describing it as 'competitive poetics', in a context where *parôle*, aided by microphones as an extension of the corporeal, 'dazzles, seduces and destroys', amounting to 'verbal lovemaking', firmly hinging on 'glorious, pyrotechnic words' (Brantley 2020). Perhaps unsurprisingly given the concept of the production, reviews of *When We Have Sufficiently Tortured Each Other* brimmed with references to the boldly erotic, specifically BDSM-driven narrative of the staging. The BDSM concept did respond to the fierce sexual play that develops in the text itself, especially when we consider the plurality of the definition itself, as developed here by cultural anthropologist Margot Weiss: 'The terms *SM* and *BDSM* [emphasis original] are used interchangeably to denote a diverse community that includes aficionados of bondage, domination/submission, pain or sensation play, power exchange, leathersex, roleplaying, and fetishes' (Weiss 2011: vii). As the production pursued such a concept throughout, the verbal was rather eclipsed by the visual, even though it is no less potent than in *Cyrano*. Jamie Lloyd's *Cyrano* was also visceral, but its power emanated through voice in a pulsating body that found no release from its craving of another.

It is important to note that neither of these productions, however different, were bound to the canon; neither was a period piece, as, most certainly, Crimp's respective texts are not either. On the contrary, both are highly modern in diction, as is also the case with Crimp's previous forays into the historical dramatic canon. The playwright, then, is dealing with tangled emotions and complex corporealities neither by tracing the archaeologies of feelings and sexualities, nor by proxy, or disembodied context. Rather, he reaches into the diachronic and – once more – the primal, and does so forensically, by capturing the embodied intricacies that connect humans across space and time. In the process, he elucidates their bearing on the human condition, on how one relates to self and others, especially where power distribution is shifting and ambivalent. The two plays discussed here, therefore, are not relics, but, as I hope to demonstrate, astute representations of conquest, domination and consumption by a force greater than oneself in the twenty-first century.

Mouths and Bodies

In *When We Have Sufficiently Tortured Each Other*, conquest is a game; its outcomes are uncertain, risqué, even outright dangerous. The subject fluctuates with uncertainty, undergoing turmoil, and testing the limits of self and Other equally, in a process of constant flow of identity, because it is sexual domination that determines the viability, and even tenability, of self. In *Cyrano de Bergerac*, beyond existential woes on the mental and emotional sphere, desire is a matter of life and death: one endangers oneself physically in a way that actually entails threat to survival. And while this could serve as a metaphor for the levels of exposure involved in any act of opening up oneself to a potential lover verbally and physically, Crimp also probes the link between surrendering to feeling and mortality; in that sense, the annihilating powers of being dominated become fully manifest.

When We Have Sufficiently Tortured Each Other is informed by a text where the drive to dominate the object of one's desire leads all action: the pursuit is relentless, and unequal. This state of 'the chase' is captured in both the form and content of Crimp's text, but the partners are given equal agency; most importantly, the text paints both characters' relentless pursuit of pleasure in such a way that guarantees 'the consensual exchange of power' (Weiss ix). The play consists of twelve scenes, which breathlessly intersect with one another; it features declarations of love and lust and fierce resulting negotiations of power. The main characters are Woman and Man – gone are the named protagonists in Richardson's fiction; the game, in Crimp, becomes primal and the designatory attributes assigned to the lead roles reflect this – at the same time, no such thing as gender binarism exists, as I go on to discuss. The intertextual referentiality of the text, and its playfulness, are such that familiar names are dropped in-text on occasion: the Man does make a reference to the Woman as Pamela, for example. The remaining characters, appearing only in specific parts of the play – at least in Crimp's text, if not in Mitchell's production, where their presence on stage was considerably more prominent – are Girl 1 and Girl 2; Mrs Jewkes; and Ross. These secondary characters serve as props, outlandishly appearing out of context in key moments; focus never wavers from the central couple, who are the primary proprietors of the exhilarating rhythm and verbal vigour of Crimp's text. They are also, of course, the primary perpetrators of the emotionally, verbally and sexually transgressive acts that unfold. Whereas in Richardson's text the power scales tilt heavily on the side of the male protagonist (Mr B), in Crimp's play the two parties share the power – the pursuit is a game between two competent players with voracious appetites for each other, but, even more so, for control. While there is sexual fearlessness, the emotional and verbal exposure creates considerable vulnerability. It is this that must be avoided at all costs, and, to this end, sex serves as weapon. Likewise, in *Cyrano*, Roxane does not emerge either as naïve, or as a target to be pursued by men. Rather, her intellectual and verbal prowess is such that Cyrano is not only impressed, but becomes acutely aware that in his coveted lover he has met his match. The drive to conquer and impress becomes heightened on account of this recognition.

It is language, then, that emerges as a most potent tool in *When We Have Sufficiently Tortured Each Other* as text, which makes it particularly important not to impose on the play a staging that might be so laboured that it could feel artificial upon its dramaturgical structure – that might, in other words, detract and distract from the expansive imagery and visceral impact of Crimp's dialogue. The same is true of *Cyrano*. Although both plays are interested in – literally – spelling out desire, they do so in different ways: one play, as its antecedent, is invested in the allure of language, its romance – but rather than surrender to it fully, it also flirts with an attraction to the dark side (*Cyrano*); the other play traces the ferocity of lust. If the former teases the seemingly inexhaustible source of new ways to describe love, lust, and devotion (*Cyrano*) the other follows, with the same tension and unwavering focus, the verbal ping-pong game between two characters captivated by the capacities of the erotic, and especially its inherent threats. Both games gravitate around not getting caught; it is the intrigue of the pursuit that prevails and the command of the lover so desired, first through words, then through the body. The desired Other, after all, embodies the ideal projection of self: strong, powerful, longed for. Without the verbal game, the web of intrigue these characters have woven – the personas they have concocted for themselves – collapses; reality, in the form of the desired Other's attainment, arguably, can never quite match the excitement, however satisfactory its fruit might appear in the precise moment of conquest.

Both plays examined in this chapter are intertextually connected to source narratives with an epistolary core, which, by extension, also establishes a further form of connection between the two Crimp texts themselves. These are, moreover, two plays profoundly engaged with desire, which, however, they do not confine to the physical; rather, they conceptualize it as a state that is mediated through the verbal. This also affords the body greater agency: beyond performing its sexual urge, it affirms itself as contextualizing this in real time, as attempting to control it, even when acknowledging, verbally, that ultimately it may never be able to do so, or not fully. 'There was always a danger of seeing the human subject as a blank sheet of paper [...] on which the social inscribed its signs', writes Jeffrey Weeks (2011: 21), while also noting that 'Bodies are objects of social practice, in the sense that they are acted upon, and inscribed with meaning; and agents in social practice' (2011: 6). I am intrigued by the lexicon Weeks uses here, one that effectively takes us into the territory of the body's *writability*, not only on the basis of the narrative that one may choose for themselves, but, also, of one that might be externally imposed – including, as is the concern of this book, in frameworks of desire and its performance, as well as its sexual expression.

The body as 'a blank sheet of paper', one to be 'inscribed with meaning', of course speaks to the power of the beholder. The process becomes fascinating when it becomes mutual: when, that is, the written-about subject begins to enact their own writing and inscribing unto others, of their own desire; or, when that same subject intercepts the ways in which they have been written about by others, so that they might potentially disrupt them; or, indeed, finally, when the subject demands that they be inscribed upon – as in written about – exercising their own agency so as to instigate the process of inscription. These are all states that we encounter in the plays this chapter is concerned with. The epistolary form encourages and enables the expansiveness of reference that we find in Crimp; the letter, in its various formats, has, after all, traditionally served as a vehicle for containing the seemingly uncontainable: love, longing, lust. Depending on the writer's capabilities, the frame of reference by far surpasses the limitations of the format – and Crimp, in both texts, creates storytellers whose narratorial finesse reigns supreme. The format of the plays facilitates expressive maximalism, without, however, stretching; the references are simultaneously precise and unrestrained – in Crimp's theatre, these are not antithetical terms.

When We Have Sufficiently Tortured Each Other: Lust as Process and Product

In *When We Have Sufficiently Tortured Each Other*, it is expression that serves both as method and as objective: domination, that is, occurs most effectively in language over any other form. 'There is a fragile complementarity between the sexes', writes Weeks, adding that, if we adopt a 'broader view' then 'desire is polymorphous and polyvocal, female as well as male, homosexual as well as heterosexual, perverse as well as "normal". The problem lies not in desire, but in the structures (psychic and social) in which it plays' (39). The observation strikes me as particularly pertinent to this, in my view one of Crimp's most slippery to account for plays, not least because of what I would describe as discord between the text and the very emphatic premiere production – even in a context where a premiere production is always emphatic by default due to the imprint it makes on a new play. The fleshing out of the 'polyvocal' within the epistolary framework is significant, because of course the play is structured on expansive fragments of narrations and differing opinions on the relationship – sexual, but not only – at the heart of the text: that between the so-called Woman and Man. But this is also a play about the 'polymorphous' and altering shapes that one and the same person might adopt, fluctuating in sexual preference, identity, and/or gender.

For the purposes of this argumentation, I would like to consider, for example, the following excerpts, purposefully not invasively condensed for brevity. As stated earlier, power is distributed equally between the two main characters, Man and Woman. However, exactly who they are, or even their gender – despite their assigned descriptors – are aspects that remain fluid and indeterminate; the same is true of their sexualities. Whether in mono- or dialogical mode, the articulation of desire prevails, essentially weaponized in the battle of asserting one's authority over one's lover. It is so from the first moments of the play, which establish the textual – and sexual – dynamics between the two characters (and their different iterations):

MAN. Let's face it, Pamela: you're a child — and I'm a man. I have power and you have none. I could lock all the doors now and strip you naked — but I'm giving you the chance to come to me of your own free will. [...] What's more I have modern ideas about sex: I believe women should enjoy it [...].

[...]

WOMAN. My name's not Pamela — and look at me: I'm not a child. You say you have all the power — but where's the evidence? And the fact you 'believe' women should enjoy sex means nothing to me. What do I care what you believe about my pleasure? Go on then: lock the doors and see what happens. Show me how much power you really have.

MAN. [...] I have so much power I don't need to lock doors — any more than I need to engage with your arguments. [...] And if you were to run from this room through any of these doors you would find yourself in a room exactly the same — and if you then ran from that room through any of that room's doors you would find yourself in another room exactly the same — and so on and so on — Pamela. [...]

(Crimp 2019i: 3–4)

Further on, the references become considerably more explicit, as well as aggressive:

WOMAN. All I think about is being inside your body — to penetrate your body, that's all that counts. I've read some very long books and in those books my attention has been drawn to other things, subtle movements of thought, political events and so on, various kinds of art: music, pictures of trees and so on — so when I say that all I think about is being inside your body, it's not like I haven't thought about other kinds of pleasure — conversation — work — I've thought about them a lot and finally dismissed them — since you — your body — is all that counts — he said.

(22)

Here, it is Woman reading Man's writing aloud, as a means of, if not capturing – because the Other, the lover, is always elusive – then at least attempting to approximate them; elsewhere, 'he' reciprocates:

MAN. 'One. Penetrate. Do I accept the word penetrate? [...]'
  'Two. Bitch. Do I invite the word bitch as a description of myself? Bitch — bitch — try it in the mouth. Acceptable? [...]'
  'Three. Love. Easy to write but what's inside it? What can I see when I scan it? What's that shape? — that spike? Why has it triggered the alarm?' Why when he says love is he dragging me off and telling me to strip? [...]'
  'Four. Man crying. What use to me is a man crying? What use to me is a man who comes too soon then cries? [...]'
  'Five. My mind. Because what I really want to know is why is my mind limited to these questions? — about men — about my body. [...] And if this is how a woman writes, what kind of woman am I?'

(27)

The questioning of 'love' and sex in a fraught context such as the one that is described here is strategic: as literary scholar Lucy Alford notes, 'there are important differences between desire and love, and vigilance at their boundaries is vital to an understanding of either term' (Alford 2020: 77). Desire, here, for another's body as much as for power, may be edging out 'love', under whose overarching structure it claims to operate, but, which, at the same time, it questions as to its signification.

The questioning of agency and of one's own sensibilities, as well as their redefinition through a process of power negotiation, are no less significant and ought to be taken into account given the bold overall context of the play, both verbal and thematic. Weiss proposes that

> *D/s*, for *domination* and *submission*, refers to the explicit exchange of power. The phrase *power exchange* emphasizes that *D/s* relationships are explicitly about power (more than sensation, pain, or role play [...]), but also that they are an exchange: although dominant and submissive roles may be relatively stable, power is understood to be mobile, shared, or routed between practitioners during play.
>
> (ix)

This we see in the excerpts quoted above abundantly, beyond the production concept. In language, therefore, lies the prospect of shift: one becomes transformed when one so decides, and one so expresses. The discord between text and production that I refer to stems precisely from the muscular emphasis on characters' shifts in a way that rendered these realistic, occasionally tedious and discernible rather than conceptual and disruptive. From the BDSM costumes and games to the presence of the secondary characters/sexual partners on stage, the production moved beyond the sphere of the confessional (as in the letters) and exploratory and into the showing, a decision that, in my view, ultimately impacted the telling. After all, in Crimp's play characters write as themselves (Man and Woman, whomever we might expect these to be), but also as Others within, pursuing different sexual and sexed iterations of themselves, or adopting the voice and perspective of others in narrations, so that distinctions are forever blurred. It is so-called 'normality' and the orthodoxy of gender binaries and heterosexuality that the play consistently targets, not least in the context of a canon that has classified *Pamela* as a narrative where the male is dominant and the female, if not subservient, then certainly persecuted, rather than, it seems to me, marital tedium. Marriage figures insofar as it is exposed precisely for the fraught 'psychic and social' stage it sets up, one within which desire attempts to carve out paths of release as characters negotiate different versions of themselves, bound and unbound to each other, towards possibilities for a co-existence where one partner is not subservient to the other and the physical is, likewise, not accountable to the emotional and intellectual.

In a play that thrives on the epistolary – here, aggressive, ruthless, even – it is the very act of writing that, more than any other, brims with the physicality of domination:

MAN. Write for me — Pamela. Since you're so keen on it.
[…]
He dictates.
[…]
She starts to write.
Yes he's right
   things do inevitably improve comma
   […] the most tender comma
   most intimate things
   between a man and a woman
   inevitably improve full stop
[…]
WOMAN. […] '… when he looks at me fire runs through my body.'
(54–55)

The *D/s* process, then, may well also be physical, but, predominantly, it is verbal: it gravitates around the magnetic pole of exposing the innermost – as in the mind: it is that which is relentlessly pursued, and that which motivates the fetishization of subjugation and domination as states that either subject is both drawn to and repelled by. Discussing 'Fetish', Weeks puts forward a proposition that goes some way towards a rounder understanding of the ways in which the gender-normative narratives – to which, in his text, through the process of the resistance epistolary form Crimp offers an embodied counter-gesture in real time – of neoliberal capitalism dictate the servitudes of belonging and of ownership not only of objects, but also of people, for example, as loyal and reliable partners and/or subservient lovers. Exploring how 'fetish' constitutes essential terminology for both psychoanalytical and Marxist approaches, Weeks writes: 'what is apparent is that fetishization is a key to the understanding of the main objects of concern in both theories: the dynamic unconscious, and the dynamics of capitalist accumulation. In both cases the fetish masks the underlying, and painful reality' (57). People, then, in such relationships of acquisition, exchange and command, become material possessions – through their surrendered, conquered bodies – much in the way that objects do. Affirming one's authority over another person might be the greatest emblem of capitalist power. What Crimp's play accomplishes that is, in the neoliberalist context in which we exist, highly subversive, is to ask whether sexually charged language, beyond the tool of commoditized fetishization, can be reclaimed as pleasurable. The fetish, that is, acts as guise, but is not, ultimately, the goal; the command that these characters pursue applies to the intellectual faculties – it is this that renders it libidinous, hence its distilling in the act of writing.

Moreover, although Crimp's text cauterizes the obsessions of ownership as seen in the preposterousness of assuming one can possess another human being, the tone in which the play exposes the tedium is not quite the same as the tone the production, with its slow yet uninterrupted (as in no breaks in action, unlike the episodic/epistolary form of the play) emphasis on domestic ennui. The fetish that the text criticizes, is, in my view, a more profound one than the production, with its overemphasis on props (therefore physical objects as fetishes) and BDSM may have encouraged one to infer, at least primarily. And although there is a perspective, as Weeks notes, that treats 'Consensual BDSM [...as an act that] provides unique insights into the nature of sexual power, therapeutic and cathartic sex, revealing the nature of sexuality as ritual and play' (165), ultimately, judgements, as Weeks also notes, are difficult to arrive at because the matter is such a complex one and views vary considerably. While I recognize that the premiere production of *When We Have Sufficiently Tortured Each Other* may have perhaps attempted to engage with the potentialities of such 'ritual and play', I hesitate to deduce that there was any detectable pleasure to this – similarly, there did not seem to be any ideology or desire behind the proliferation of this 'play', but, in my spectatorial experience, merely perfunctory routine. To depict BDSM as a pointless exercise may of course be an entirely valid ideology in itself, but it does not, in my view, quite match the semantic nuances of Crimp's text, problematizing them sufficiently.

Cyrano de Bergerac: **The Sharpness Delicate**

To suggest that the singular word functions as an atom of meaning, dense and heavy with signification lingering and profound, is, perhaps, an appropriate way of capturing the attentiveness that accompanies lexical selection as we see it in Crimp's writing. This does not only concern the playwright's process: it is also reflected in the ways in which characters reach for the words, in a process that is corporeal, tangible. Some are gifted speakers – others are not, but, as I have also discussed elsewhere (Angelaki 2012: 87–120), in Crimp's plays being an accomplished handler of language is, often, a matter of life or death, metaphorically, but, also, on occasion, literally. In *Cyrano de Bergerac*, this is meant more in the latter way than in most of Crimp's other texts. Here, life is precarious: there is war, there is street violence, there are, also, the sharp edges of love itself and their potential consequences. It is in the presence of love that a mortally wounded Cyrano chooses to expire at the end of the play – the very moment in which he finally makes his confession to Roxane, fifteen years after the events that led to her husband's death – that same husband, Christian, who only secured Roxane's affections on the basis of Cyrano's words.

The plot of the source text is well-known, and it is retained in Crimp's adaptation: Cyrano, a man in Roxane's circle of trust, is asked to serve as the mediator between her and the man she is in love with. The cause for the mediation is that Christian must woo Roxane with words. The physical attraction is unquestionable; it is the intellectual one that leaves a lot to be desired, and it is precisely this that Cyrano's letters set out to ignite. Christian cannot write about love, but Roxane needs to read about it; Cyrano, on the other hand, needs an outlet for its release – he is, after all, desperately, all-consumingly in love with Roxane. So is born a *ménage à trois* sustained by poetry: Cyrano writes the letters that Christian supposedly addresses to Roxane; Roxane hears precisely how she is worshipped, unaware that Christian is merely

Cyrano's mouthpiece. Without discounting the consuming desire that feeds the fire of writing, it is, ultimately, the love of and for words that proves to be the most resilient in the play.

It is a comment that Cyrano makes early in the play that best serves to capture its essence: poetry, he says, has the capacity to 'draw blood' (Crimp 2019b: 22) and the effort is concerted, calculated; we are dealing with dexterity and intent. There are similar statements of authorial swagger, where the sharpness of language is emphasized as both a means and an end. We hear Cyrano say, for example:

> My sword is long, not so my song,
> my song is quick as steel.
>   Parry – riposte – the fight is lost
> my friend – and no appeal.
>
> (23)

Or: 'My system is simple: don't think, just let rip' (26). Cyrano is recognizable by his extraordinarily long nose as much as by his poetic talent; he may be fearless as a fighter and a writer, but he is entirely vulnerable when it comes to love. This is why, when summoned by Roxane to an early meeting that he initially misconstrues as a romantic invitation, bravado gives way to an emotional nakedness that threatens to leave him wholly exposed. Nothing that Roxane discusses, other than her fond memories of their deep-rooted kinship, proves to be the source of joy that he had longed for. For Cyrano, Roxane represents both desire and despair: as Roxane remarks, in an irony unbeknownst to her during an encounter where Cyrano, hidden from her, pretends to be Christian: '[...My words] hit their mark instantly' to which Cyrano replies: 'Because their target's broad: wide – and as open – as my heart' (71). Words can inflict injuries, yes, but, beyond this, Cyrano speaks of utter annihilation – in Roxane's speech, he lives or dies: such is the vast space of his desire, which takes the shape that her discourse will allow; within it he may feel deliriously free, or dramatically confined.

It is during this encounter that all confidence and self-preservation give way when desire becomes impossible to harness, producing, arguably, the landmark monologue of the play (again with Cyrano speaking as Christian, including his accent as McAvoy played this in the Lloyd production), cited here condensed:

CYRANO. [...] I love you, I need you, I want you, I go to sleep thinking about you and wake up with your voice winding through my head, I look at you and I can't focus, the whole world shimmers,

I'm ashamed, I'm angry, I'm in love, I'm mad, I'm happy, I'm dead, I'm alive, [...] the whole world shimmers and I burn and I burn with love –

ROXANE. Christian ...

CYRANO. – the whole world shimmers – and the night – and the sky – and your voice shimmers – I've no wit, I've no mind, I've no brake, I've no self-control, I've no shame, [...] I desire you, I write to you, I write for you, [...] I strip you, I clothe you, I do up the tiniest buttons at your sleeve, [...] I'm speechless, speechless, all I can say is I want – I want – I want – there is no poetry – there is no structure that can make any sense of this – only I want – I want – I want – I want you, Roxane.

(73–74)

Considered in its expanded form of which the above is an indication, the monologue reveals the feverish punctuation of desire, as emotion, physical urge and speech blend into one ungovernable entity, where no full-stop can interfere between Cyrano and the sentiment. McAvoy's delivery of the monologue offered the optimal physical embodiment, reminding, as Theodor Adorno once put it, that 'There is no element in which language resembles music more than in the punctuation marks' (1990: 300), or, also that

> one can sense the difference between a subjective will that brutally demolishes the rules and a tactful sensitivity that allows the rules to echo in the background even where it suspends them. This is especially evident with the most inconspicuous marks, the commas, whose mobility readily adapts to the will to expression, only, however, to develop the perfidiousness of the object, *die Tücke des Objekts*, in such close proximity to the subject and become especially touchy, making claims one would hardly expect of them.
>
> (305)

Musicality in speech, for a writer as involved and skilled in music as Crimp, is particularly meaningful, not least considering the urban culture aesthetics of the Lloyd production, attuned to the rhythms and sounds of speech as it becomes a poem, desire humming from within. Or, likewise, the slipperiness and peril of language, in those inconspicuous, yet entirely non-innocent commas, which mobilize longing, reveal a writer entirely in control of the language rule-book, so much so that he is capable of suspending it completely for the required affect. In this flow of desirous speech, unimpeded by restraint, undeterred even by the interjection of his love antagonist's name, which is spoken by Roxane, Cyrano evidences not only the full range of – to equal measure – the heavenly and hellish iterations of love that consumes mind, body, and soul, but also, its selfishness. As Alford notes, 'Perhaps the oldest and most essential mode of poetic attention is that of love and its hungrier variety, desire. Tending toward a beloved object, whether earthly or divine, is a central manifestation of transitive attention in classical and contemporary poetic contexts' (76). Here, Crimp crafts the shared space between classical and contemporary through an unruly poem that defies all metre; the beloved is both earthly and divine; such is the range of emotion that she awakens. But however transitive the attention, the 'I' is dominant: most of the phrases are led by it into the battle of conquest. It is what the subject feels, what they experience that determines the content – the Other, that so desired lover, remains a foreign land. And while the adoration is undoubtable, we need to consider whether in a torrent of speech so powerful there is any room allowed for that Other to truly interject (we see clearly that Roxane is not allowed to verbally interfere for too long, for example).

Alford theorizes longing, and distance, as potent tropes of desire: 'Add to interest an interval of distance (the experience of lack that produces the dynamic of longing), and we move one step closer to the particular dynamics of desire. [...I]n *desire* the relation is more dominantly characterized by distance, by not having' (77). Elsewhere, and of value to our understanding of the dynamic that Crimp's text establishes between Cyrano's craving, subjectivity-fuelled speech and Roxane as addressee, both present and distant, an impression accentuated in the production, where, even though seated in close proximity on a bare set, the suspension of disbelief requires us to imagine a physical obstacle between them that hinders proximity, Alford elaborates on the importance of the subjective position to the articulation of desire:

> In the poetry of both love and desire, the attentional lens is focalized—[...] so that the object fills most of the attentional field, and the ground recedes. Yet because of the heightened degree of interest, [...] the subject's consciousness of its own standing in relation (either of distance or of proximity) to the object cuts into the attentional centrality of the object: I attend not only to the object on its own, in and of itself, but also to my own subjective position, my feelings for it, my longing, my distance, my proximity, my lack.
>
> (89)

What we see in Crimp's text above, then, is the solitary journey of longing, infused with the pain, and the fascination, of 'not having'. In that space, the Other is conceptualized as much as the de facto prerequisite for fulfilment, as she is extrinsic to that very fulfilment.

Still, there is nothing passive about this. As Alford notes, 'The relation between I and thou, or between I and an absence of a though [...] is also the seat of what can be understood as the primary ethical or relational dynamic [...]. Both contemplation and desire involve the subject's attentive reach towards its object, the subject filling with its object, perhaps even dissolving or growing porous in the act of attending to another' (76). Desire, that is, is equally root, process, and destination. This we can deduce from the sound and appearance of the text: the constant dashes and commas create the effect of a moving force that gathers momentum, uncontrolled as much as unimpeded. The confession is breathless, and the addressee is as much the idealized lover as the speaking subject themselves: this is a register, a 'love log' that is, which, beyond demanded by that Other, is now essential for its very speaker. Indeed, the trance and the spell are never broken, as syntax and punctuation show: there is no pausing for reflection, no rhyme for 'poetry', no 'structure' for reason. There is, exactly as Cyrano says, no ordering and no 'brake', whether in language or feeling. It is language that consumes the body, and language that also sustains it.

While language exists, Cyrano survives, defiant of danger and of his enemies. Roxane is the ideal that, unattainable, furnishes his repertoire with inspiration. It is not a process dissimilar to that which we see in *When We Have Sufficiently Tortured Each Other*: the verbal game sustains the desire and vice versa. 'Dazzle me with language', urges Roxane; this is the challenge – or 'talk the talk' as Christian puts it, to which Cyrano retorts: 'Talk the talk? Do you not mean set on fire the obscure object of your heart's yet still more obscure desire?' (55). *Cyrano* is not a more innocent text than *When We Have Sufficiently Tortured Each Other*, nor does it deal with aspects of desire more noble than the latter – if anything, both texts show us that there is nothing noble about desire, which, here, is often interwoven with deception. As in *When We Have Sufficiently Tortured Each Other* the two protagonists/antagonists forever concoct games so as to prevail over each other, so in *Cyrano* there is a process of active manipulation at play: Roxane's emotions are handled by others, and she becomes, unbeknownst to her, alienated from her own desire, which is displaced from the man she believes to be its receptor, to the man for whom she feels no – or at least not consciously – physical attraction. At the same time, the power of language to handle and enchant leaves no part of the love triangle unaffected:

Christian's final words, to which I return in the next section, arguably the most poetic he speaks in the duration of the play, voice an unfulfilled desire that, when expressed, allows the body to surrender to its own annihilation.

Fluidities Sexual and Intertextual

As Christian – the man that the source text, as well as subsequent versions, overwhelmingly cast as the eponymous hero's love rival – is mainly seen to fulfil a specific catalytic role in the structure of the narrative, his own desire is too often relegated to an event of lesser significance. The assumed spectatorial – or readerly – position is that one wants Cyrano to prevail in this battle of words, in this war of emotions; and so Christian is, eventually, sidelined. Not so in Crimp's *Cyrano*, where Christian's desire is presented as thoroughly unpredictable, with potential to disturb, because this, too, is the kind of desire that a society that has not yet embraced difference would vilify. As Christian and Cyrano have a charged confrontation in the later part of the play, what this culminates in is not a claiming of Roxane's affections, but, rather, the following confession:

CHRISTIAN. I don't know. Is there a version of life where two men can
   live as one person?
   Christian kisses Cyrano – tentatively at first, but with increasing intensity.
   Then backs away.
   No … No …

(107)

There is such tenderness in the moment of utterance, and, at the same time, such resolute and profound recognition that on the basis of the prevailing heteronormative structures and staunch performances of masculinity – not least amongst soldiers, which both characters are – the very thought would have been inconceivable; the act impossible. Masculinities, however, Crimp's *Cyrano* shows us, are multitudinous; love, affection, and desire can no longer be heteronormatively conceptualized, regardless of the canonical root of the source narrative. For a contemporary piece of theatre to be not only resonant but also responsible – in the sense not of moralistic instructivism but of feeling the tone of its own socio-spatial context and actively advancing these discourses, we need to move forward more resolutely. Crimp's *Cyrano* performs this change.

   When We Have Sufficiently Tortured Each Other recognizes shifts, too. Gone is the tenuous virtue of the female, the master-slave agenda driven by the virile male. Here, it is not only what 'female' and 'male' might stand for today that is thrust into doubt, but also, the assumption that they might exist at all. There are such appropriations of another's voice, gender-bending and gender-defying that we witness across the play, that 'subject' becomes a flowing signifier along with 'identity' and 'sexuality'. Eventually, we reach a most caustically humorous and anti-climactic finale (at least in the text). The very title of the closing scene, 'When It Comes to Picnics', is suggestive of this:

Man and Woman only. A few toys for young children may be scattered about.
WOMAN. (*smiles*) What?
[...]
MAN. Well you seem to be thinking that if it was you who'd got everything ready – the food, I mean, and the children – you'd've done it much quicker. It's not that you're angry – just that you assume you're superior. That's also your attitude to other things.

(74)

The dialogue continues along these lines, deepening in comical effect, as more examples are introduced of the antagonistic domestic relationship concerning the distribution of chores and power dynamics between the couple. A distinctive lack of affection is visible, heightening the artificiality of the relationship that is crafted on minutiae, but does not carry any emotional substance of observable depth. And while the most probable initial assumption begins to set in, namely, that Crimp's text is subverting gender structures by reversal of the traditionalist model and by making the female/mother/'Woman' character into the assertive partner, while the male/father/'Man' character becomes the subjugated partner, a further reversal occurs that is considerably more intricate, and that solidifies what it is that firmly moves us, as the play enters its very final stretch, into resolutely Crimp territory. Specifically:

MAN. The thing is … is I feel you're not really listening to me. And I hate to say this but I think the reason you're not listening is because I'm a woman.

(77)

Whether this elaborate role-play (including an indignant, perhaps staged resistance to the turn instigated by the 'Man' character from the 'Woman' character, as follows) is the writer's nod to a radical neo-absurdism that texts like *In the Republic of Happiness* have previously begun to explore, or not, by now all sense of gender fixity has been thoroughly compromised and suitably disposed of.

Perhaps Mitchell's approach to the scene where, as the show closes, we see the character played by the female lead attach an artificial penis (or 'strap-on') and prepare to penetrate the anus of the character played by the male lead, was a way of highlighting this fluidity in a manner more applied. It strikes me, however, that the poetry of Crimp's text, where in the most subversive and yet quietest of ways heteronormativity and gender-based supremacy are resolutely dismantled while operating in the framework of another of the institutions that the play queries as a concept – family – is not given the conceptual space to unfold here. The visual steerage of the production is, arguably, too hectic to allow for this. Weeks observes that 'As sensitivity to the ways in which sexuality is shaped on the fluid boundaries of the biological, the psychological and socio-historical grows, it is likely that the concept of hybridity will continue to be valuable in theorizing such rich and varied patterns' (91). This is a helpful claim towards contextualizing the dialectical representational process of which *Cyrano de Bergerac* and *When We Have Sufficiently Tortured Each Other* form part and that speaks to the normative continuities – and disruptions to these – that the texts are also conversant with. This is especially so when it comes to Weeks's mention of 'the fluid boundaries of the [...] socio-historical', both in terms of its narrativization – open rather than fixed, through intertextual channels such as those that Crimp explores – and the re-interpretative and therefore re-constitutive acts of both the literary and the historical canon (a flow, rather than a closed book), delivered by works such as those examined in this chapter. Certainly, however, particularly when it comes to the 'socio-historical' implications relating to the political, the observation applies to the texts that the following chapter takes on as well. Weeks additionally observes that 'The term hybridity, like so much in the conceptualization of sexuality, has its roots in nineteenth-century botanical and biological language. It suggests a cross-fertilization of natural elements to create a new entity (as with plants and animal breeds)' (90). The marital formation that Crimp explores in *When We Have Sufficiently Tortured Each Other*, in which the partners blend into a novel iteration constituted of both in their fluid gender and sexuality forms, while, at the same time, retaining the core of a union, impresses me as particularly relevant to the ecologies of such a description.

Closing Reflections

It is in such dramaturgical acts, I argue, where Crimp's interventionist intertextuality hinges. For this, both plays examined in this chapter can serve as examples: Crimp is in dialogue with, but never merely replicates the source texts, and even though he pays heed to the textual sensibilities of the existing materials, that is, their inner narrative threads, Crimp is not in thrall to these. Ultimately, the work is geared to the contemporary theatre spectator: the theatre carrying the liveness of a forum that thrives on presence, and, therefore, on all of the resulting corporeal and affective – in the sense of emotional, intellectual, and physical – parameters at play at the same time. We recognize the connections to Rostand's *Cyrano* and Richardson's *Pamela*, respectively; but Crimp's variegated approach guarantees that we are not, as audience, brought to an installation where the literary canon performs itself for us, while our role is to affirm and proliferate its valour. While attentive and intuitive when it comes to the source texts, Crimp also secedes from the venerated masterpieces. As in the Vermeer piece, of which Crimp writes with such indelible affinity in *The Art of Painting*, the work is forever a flow: both captured on the page and a product of research, revision, and reinterpretation; tentative, ultimately, in the sense that it is never safe, that it is forever part of a conversation that unfolds with the contemporary spectator/citizen in real time – and even though it resists inspective explication, its forensic clarity remains uncontested.

In the final moments of Crimp's *Cyrano de Bergerac*, Roxane, having learned the truth as to the authorship of the letters that she believed Christian had been writing to her, burns one of them emphatically in front of Cyrano. Unbeknownst to her, he is in his final moments, grievously injured. Roxane's wrath turns violent, and the words become the target. In his letters, Cyrano has handled Christian's love with care; he has also, from his perspective, handled Roxane with care, catering to her needs – writing the words she had longed to hear. Moreover, in what could be considered an act of both self-care, that is, preservation, a mode of continuing his relationship with Roxane without risking the consequences of truth, and lack of care towards the self at the same time, in that by remaining in the orbit of her relationship with Christian, he experienced first-hand the tenderness that he would never become the recipient of himself, Cyrano negotiated his own love. The attention to the minutiae of Roxane, as captured, for example, in the sentence 'I do up the tiniest buttons at your sleeve' (74) that she now references back to him angrily (124), is the kind of care that Cyrano also exercises towards the vehicle for the words: the object that carries the love – the letter. Roxane's feelings of frustration, humiliation, even, lead her to the burning of the letter, the words given to the fire that Cyrano had described in that very letter referenced. Cyrano, unable to intercept the act, faint, pleads repeatedly 'Please don't do that / to the letter' (123). The call to protection is emphatic: it is not the feelings themselves, but the words that ought to be shielded. It is those that have been handled delicately – those that ought to be preserved, even after, as is the case with Cyrano, their writer has perished. In *When We Have Sufficiently Tortured Each Other*, the sentiment is a similar one: bodies and feelings are not spared – as in *Cyrano de Bergerac*, anything can happen to the body. It can be tested by love, by sex, by power, by abuse – but the words the body speaks are of the utmost importance. Such is, ultimately, the affect that the epistolary device at the centre of both narratives serves to deliver, heart, to hand, to mouth.

Notes

1. All references to the performance refer to my experience of the live show on 9 February 2019.
2. All references to the performance refer to my experience of the live show on 23 February 2022 at the Harold Pinter Theatre (London), where the original 2019 production, with some cast changes, opened following the COVID-19 theatre closures period.

Bibliography

Adorno, T. W. (1990) 'Punctuation Marks', translated by S. W. Nicholsen, *The Antioch Review* 48(3), pp. 300–305.

Alford, L. (2020) *Forms of Poetic Attention*. New York: Columbia University Press.

Angelaki, V. (2012) *The Plays of Martin Crimp: Making Theatre Strange*. Basingstoke: Palgrave Macmillan.

Brantley, B. (2020) 'Review: James McAvoy's Rapping Cyrano Dazzles with Words'. Available at: https://www.nytimes.com/2020/01/08/theater/cyra-no-london-review.html (Accessed: 12 Sept. 2020).

Crimp, M. (2019b) *Cyrano de Bergerac – Freely Adapted from the Play by Edmond Rostand*. London: Faber & Faber.

Crimp, M. (2019i) *When We Have Sufficiently Tortured Each Other: Twelve Variations on Samuel Richardson's Pamela*. London: Faber & Faber.

Green, A. I. (2011) 'Playing the (Sexual) Field: The Interactional Basis of Systems of Sexual Stratification', *Social Psychology Quarterly*, 74(3), pp. 244–266.

Richardson, S. (2001) *Pamela; or, Virtue Rewarded*. Oxford: Oxford University Press.

Rostand, E. (2012) *Cyrano de Bergerac*. Hamburg: Tredition Classics.

Weeks, J. (2011) *The Languages of Sexuality*. London: Routledge.

Weiss, M. (2011) *Techniques of Pleasure: BDSM and the Circuits of Sexuality*. Durham: Duke University Press.

4 Falling Tragically

The Rest Will Be Familiar to You from Cinema and Lessons in Love and Violence

It is difficult, perhaps, to imagine two forms of representational art more challenging than ancient Greek tragedy and opera. Even though each genre is different from the other and certainly distinct, what they share is their ability to incite high emotion precisely because of the way in which they delve into the greatest pathos, into the core of what it is that constitutes humanity. There is a very specific geometry to these texts: the lines are precise, the structure sharp – and within such parameters the most extravagant of transgressions unfold, and the most irreconcilable of desires take shape. Martin Crimp has, by now, an established record of successful engagement with both tragedy and opera, in productions that have garnered him considerable praise as well as international recognition for the particularly astute way in which he negotiates the challenges of the respective genres with a view to delivering timelessness as well as contemporaneity. This is, arguably, what makes Crimp's writing such an excellent partner to these genres: even though his language is conceptually maximalist and his thematic canvas expansive, there is still no excess in any verbal or formal sense. This precision of language that does not digress, and yet captures the full horizon of human activity and emotion, is, ultimately, the most astute tool for representing behavioural excess – not least of those in positions of power, whose personal digressions have, as this chapter goes on to discuss, direct civic consequences. Both works examined in this chapter, *The Rest Will Be Familiar to You from Cinema*[1] and *Lessons in Love and Violence*[2] serve as manifestations of the by-default reciprocity of the private and public realms.

Inciting High Emotion

As far as the focal areas of this book are concerned, the texts examined in this chapter give us a very considerable amount of material to draw on, so the ensuing analysis will be suitably selective. Both

DOI: 10.4324/9781003033400-5

pieces are also intertextual paradigms: *The Rest Will Be Familiar to You from Cinema* is an adaptation of *The Phoenician Women* (or *Phoenissae*) by Euripides; for *Lessons in Love and Violence*, the prototext is history itself, but as specific literary precursors are concerned, the closest connection would be to Christopher Marlowe's *Edward II*. In both cases, Crimp revisits the existing narrative from an interventionist perspective: not to rewrite history, but to reinscribe within it the human vein, for all its imperfections but, also, its possibilities, and for all its transgressions, but, also, its self-sacrifices. The sexualities engaged with in these respective works are also remarkably nuanced, accentuating that desire, and to an extent love – insofar as it is this emotion that we encounter in these plays – has no singular identity, and that one form of relationship cannot claim hierarchy over another, not even in the stateliest of contexts. Desire is also given some of its finer nuances in these works, covering, among other experiences, the virginal; the marital and extramarital; the incestuous; the repressed – as well as their gradiences and intersections that reveal the all-consuming nature of the emotion, and its unique ability to act as both a galvanizing and destructive force.

The two pieces examined in this chapter share an international trajectory as far as their staging histories are concerned, and while this is a common characteristic connecting much of Crimp's work, it is significant to identify this particular thread on the basis of the archetypal stories at hand: politics, power, destruction. In both texts, the root of destruction is desire, and specifically male desire – an indication of the hubristic arrogance of the male leader, which manifests itself in the personal and political alike. In *The Rest Will Be Familiar to You from Cinema* we see the aftermath of desire passed down from father to son (Laios, then Oedipus), whose recipient is the same woman (Jocasta): wife, mother, wife, mother, in a vicious cycle that ultimately delivers downfall and despair.[3] Two marriages collapse, with the same bride at the epicentre of political crisis. First, Jocasta is wife to Laios; subsequently, and unwittingly, to their son, Oedipus. Around this minefield different points of injury and trauma arise, as no one is left unaffected; there is no such thing as a happy union, no state that allows one to negotiate the needs of the self in a way that enables them to fathom the needs of another as equally significant. In a text with this tangled a weave of relationships – not least familial – each character's path is, ultimately, only solitary. The same holds true in *Lessons in Love and Violence*: the King's decision to surrender power and authority to the man – Gaveston – who is the object of his devotion, and also his lust, may appear selfless, but it is the pursuit of desire that drives the decision; the need to satisfy a certain part of the self, the body, that betrays another, the mind. And, yet, there is no such thing as a binary: the King knows all along that the relationship will seal his doom, but he refuses to intervene in the course of the affair. This is a relationship not built on equal terms, but not on the grounds that we might expect either: we might think that it is the King that is the powerful one; but it is Gaveston with whom the authority in the affair firmly rests. The King's political self-preservation, ultimately, fades against his personal self-sustenance. The former is strategic, and rational; the latter is sexual, and irrational.

Both productions, directed by Katie Mitchell, offered highly memorable visual environments, owing equally to Mitchell's work and to that of the scenographers attached in each case: Alex Eales in *The Rest Will Be Familiar to You from Cinema* and Vicki Mortimer in *Lessons in Love and Violence*. The scale was suitably epic: royal residences, imposing, grandiose – however given to disarray; however much they served as the canvas for destruction. Their poetry, in dark and decaying hues for the former; in bright royal blues for the latter, both underlined and accentuated the story. The productions might impress one as interconnected, despite their differences, not only by means of the electrified historical wire that they pursue, whose diachronic relevance vibrates into the present with resonances that I shall go on to address, but, also, because of the space they create, responsively and intuitively, for music. In the case of *Lessons in Love and Violence*, the complementation is mutual: the text is not subservient to the music, nor does the music overwhelm the text – such is the essence of Crimp and Benjamin's balanced partnership as it has developed over time, from the early days of *Into the Little Hill*, to *Written on Skin*, to the more recent work discussed here. In the case of *The Rest Will Be Familiar to You from Cinema*, it is Crimp who introduces the musical interjections in the form of considerate inclusions that claim their own space, rather than serving as mere accompaniment to the plot (for a discussion of music in Crimp's work, see also Angelaki 2012). The Mozart and Bach pieces that Crimp integrates, written into the script rather than transposed by the production, are as dense with the weight and signification of the historical canon as the events of the play itself. The complementation is subtle and robust at the same time, and emotion is suitably heightened through the musicscape, or, as Crimp describes the Bach aria 'Die Seele ruht in Jesu Händen', 'The plaintive oboe melody cuts through the texture of staccato recorders and pizzicato bass' (2019g: 54). 'In what kind of world was this music written?' asks one of the Girls (54), the Phoenician women who, more than a Chorus, are the superstructural actor narrators who drive the events we witness, both part of, and above the plot characters' drama (see also Angelaki 2014). It is a woman who wonders about the music – who attempts to connect that essence (the sound) which transcends the human, to the – always reduced – reality of human experience, played against a canvas of confines against desire. It is a sentiment with which Crimp's characters also grapple in *Lessons in Love and Violence*, their personal – and political – crises unfolding, vocalized in song, as their human fallibility sinks them to the seabed, eventually eliminating them. This is the feeling for which Mortimer's [the designer, rather than the character in this opera] gradually draining aquarium, visible during the performance, provided the most ideal metaphor. Characters here, too, are unable to reach the divinity that they might so desire for themselves; the one that would extricate and expiate them from history, lifting them above the structure of the narrative, to which they are, nonetheless, irretrievably bound; the tension in the music captures this very state – its eerie loftiness embodies it. Music is, after all, also a text, and Crimp's intertextuality is complex and dense.

Music, then, is a component in itself, an agent and a force – a presence, and even an ally. When, for example, in *The Rest Will Be Familiar to You from Cinema*, Antigone is asked by her Minder why she is late, and why her sister, Ismene, is still missing, Antigone replies: 'Ismene can't come. She's got music' (15). Women, and of course girls, as typically in Crimp's work, are always at the forefront: agents of action and receivers of the actions of others, which they never, however, *not* counteract; to which they never surrender. Antigone is about to experience what it means to transition from girlhood to womanhood as a person who has to negotiate her own changing views of the world and of those around her, in the context of a family crisis so radical that it is both private and public. Yet, we never do see Ismene in the play; Ismene's desire is music, and so she is at her lesson. Defiant, Antigone delivers the line that protects her sister; the music becomes a texture, an entity, a shield; music preserves Ismene from crisis, at least for the moment.

Desire and/or Marriage

One of the most poignant sites of intersection between the two texts and productions comes in the female leads: fallen queens, prey to their own desires (for a man, or for power) but also to the desires of men, which impact them directly and indirectly – and for which they develop counteraction strategies, with varying degrees of control, or success. It is these axons, then, that the chapter concentrates on: desire that is gendered; its urges and repercussions; and marriage as the ultimate problematic structure that, alternatingly: is compelled by blind desire; fails to provide a structure for desire; proves insufficient as a vehicle for desire that leads to radical alienation for the individual. As this chapter embarks on its main analytical focus, I am particularly drawn to Jeffrey Weeks's historical contextualization of marriage as both concept and reality:

> The historian John Boswell has compared marriage in pre-modern Europe with marriage in the modern West. In the earlier period, he argues, marriage conventionally began as a property arrangement, in its middle was chiefly about raising children, and ended about love. Western marriage, on the other hand, begins about love, in its middle is still largely about raising children, and often ends about property – 'by which point love is absent or a distant memory' (Boswell 1994: xxii). Despite (or perhaps because of) the rather disenchanted tone, Boswell is suggesting several highly significant points. First, marriage, generally seen as a universal of human history, and widely touted as the cornerstone of Western societies – the seventeenth-century philosopher John Locke called marriage humankind's 'first society' – has changed its meanings and implications dramatically over time. Marriage is not a fixed, stable institution.
>
> (107)

Such observations are particularly relevant to the focus of this chapter, due to the densely historical context of the specific texts, as well as the archetypal character of the marriages at their core, which Crimp's intertextual intervention serves to unsettle, to undermine. It does so not by accepting humans as at the mercy of fate, of forces greater than themselves, to which they must fall prey for humanity to progress, as it were, or to learn its lessons, its *epimythia*. Rather, it imagines the players at the heart of these (hi)stories as agents, making choices about their fate, active even in their ignorance, because this can never be fully claimed.

As such, these characters are presented as aware of the potentially catastrophic consequences of desire. It is precisely because of this awareness, and the fact that they make the choices that produce their downfall anyway, that Crimp's texts emerge as such significant literary acknowledgments of the fact that desire is a monumental force. No choice is ever decorporealized, regardless of individual levels of responsibility and/or authority; that 'fire' that Julia talks about in *Men Asleep*, or that Cyrano exalts in the eponymous play, can, ultimately, never be quite extinguished. In its wake, it, alone, has the power to claim any-one, and anything. Beyond the didactic, Crimp's texts serve to revivify that which cannot be filed away, or archived, because it is always alive: the humanity at the epicentre of history; and at the epicentre of that humanity, we find lust. Despite attempts at circumscribing artificial linearities across different historical periods, then, the ensuing analysis proceeds from the ending of the above quotation: 'Marriage is not a fixed, stable institution'. Crimp's texts, examined here, serve to inter-textually inject that very *peripeteia* of desire in the stories we thought we knew. In doing so, Crimp restores them to their human core – claiming equal space for flesh as for mind.

In its original review following the 2013 premiere, *Nachtkritik* described the lead character of Iokaste (Jocasta) as the 'engaged representative of rea-son' ['engagierte Anwältin der Vernunft und Staatsraison'] (Spatz 2019), both in the sense of individual and collective; simultaneously representing citizen and state. Such a description speaks directly to Jocasta's duality as wife and stately figure, and her consequent, perennial oscillation between the private and public domains. In its review of the play's 2019 produc-tion at the Münchner Volkstheater, the *Abendzeitung* describes Jocasta as 'strict parent, loving mother, attentive but ultimately failing intermediary in the conflict of the brothers [...her two sons, Eteocles and Polynices, both aggressive in their battle for head of state] and equally woman on the verge of a nervous breakdown' ['liebende Mutter, aufmerksame aber schließlich scheiternde Vermittlerin im Streit der Brüder, der ein poli-tischer Konflikt wird, und Frau am Rande des Nervenzusammenbruchs zugleich'] (Hejny 2019). The female element in Crimp's work is, after all, and enduringly, strong – a point proven emphatically in his radical adaptations (examples include not only the texts examined in this chap-ter, but, also, other work, most notably 2004's *Cruel and Tender*). These feature irreverent intertextual dialogues between present and past, across histories actual and imagined, all the while undermining the dominance of established narratives towards a re-conceptualization of the human project, and of women at its beating heart.

Elsewhere, discussing *Lessons in Love and Violence*, reviewers have been astute in their underlining of a theme that allows me to estab-lish an intertextual link between the two texts covered in this chap-ter within the body of Crimp's work: 'The story encompasses both a dysfunctional royal family whose misrule causes misery to its subjects, and a convoluted sadomasochistic sexual relationship between the king and his lover. Big questions are raised about public versus private, art versus life' (Church 2018). Such a remark establishes an interesting link to *When We Have Sufficiently Tortured Each Other* in terms of the nature of the erotic relationship; the remainder of the comment is also significant, as it is wholly applicable to *The Rest Will Be Familiar to You from Cinema*. Further assessments such as that 'The title may separate its two concepts – Lessons in Love and Violence – but what we're really unpicking here (what we're always unpicking with these two authors) is the fleshy tangle of the two, the stubbornly indivisible [...] love and violence' also resonate (Coghlan 2018). The binary evaporates; the experience is entirely visceral – because such is the nature of desire, all consuming, whether for a lover, or for control, or indeed both; in political power, too, there is an element of the erotic and the fetishist; and in Crimp's texts desire is entirely about power. As one reviewer adds, 'For over a decade now, and over the course of three collaborations [the other being *Into the Little Hill* and *Written on Skin*], the composer and playwright have been teaching us their lessons – serving up operatic parables on power, politics, desire and the darkest urges of human nature' (Coghlan 2018).

One of the most insightful reviews of *Lessons in Love and Violence* establishes the theme that I find to be dominant in both texts: that 'love can lead to disastrous choices, especially for those in power' (Fearn 2018). For the King love is whole, uncategorizable, unconquerable – indeed, also, in this case, ruinous. This reviewer is also entirely accurate in suggesting that the 'King follows his desires with a ruthless sense of entitlement' (Fearn 2018). The King is distracted, then side-tracked from his responsibilities towards his subjects; his surrender to the object of his affection is complete, and unequivocal. For example:

KING. How can I love you?
    A man with the steel hand
    and sleepy smile on an assassin.
GAVESTON. Yes I'm a human razor:
    take care or I'll cut your throat.
KING. You bite your fingernails like a boy does –
    the skin's broken where you punched the wall –
    why did you punch the wall?
GAVESTON. Love is a prison:
    I wanted to see daylight.
KING. How can I love a man who calls love a prison? –
    who says he would cut my throat?
    How would you kill me, Gaveston? –
    would it be slow? –
    or sudden?
GAVESTON. I'd only kill you for money.

                                           (Crimp 2019c: 207–208)

In denying that he can possibly describe their bond as one of love, the King effectively confirms that this is how he feels towards Gaveston, becoming increasingly desperate for his lover's generosity, or some form of tenderness – bur none is forthcoming. The King is awake to the risk, but, also, unable to contain it. We are, ultimately, in the territory of Freud, and the tension between *Eros* and *Thanatos*; Gaveston, the King fears, while also being fascinated, will bring about his death.

I would like, here, to turn to the work of theatre scholar Karoline Gritzner. Even though Gritzner does not write about Crimp's work specifically, I find that her engagement with layered, and, to an extent, uncategorizable storytelling for the stage – distinct, yet not unlike Crimp's in its overall elusiveness and strangeness, serves the purposes of this discussion, not least in its engagement with the non-binary pair of death and desire, especially in a context of historical intertextuality. As Gritzner notes:

> Mythology tells us that love, sexual desire and death co-exist as conflicting yet complementary forces in the human psyche. Theatre and theory, from the ancient world to the present day, have explored the embodiments and conceptual constellations of sexuality, desire and death in a multitude of ways. Sigmund Freud [...] distinguishes two classes of instincts which exist in an opposing yet complementary relationship: the life instincts (Eros) and the death drive (Thanatos). [...] Eros is self-preserving and life-creating desire [...]. The sexual instincts are counterbalanced by the death drive, whose aim is destruction [...].
>
> (2010: 2)

As Gritzner underlines in a dismantling of the binary, 'Despite the dualistic presentation of both kinds of drive, Freud emphasised that they exist in a relationship of interdependence and fusion' (2). The two works by Crimp examined in this chapter hinge on the archetypal by means of their universality, as well as of their historical depth. Crimp's radical updating and retelling, in terms of both form and content, render evident the grounds on which these stories bear such significance not only for our past, but also for our present and future, mirrors of the human condition.

The hypothesis that Gritzner presents in her analysis is verifiable in both texts examined in this chapter. Firstly, it applies to the King and Gaveston, but, also, to the King and Isabel (his spouse and queen). The King, that is, appears determined to experience the joy of his relationship with Gaveston, as well as the possibilities of his rule through a deviation from the norm that his bond with Gaveston, wildly dynamic and ambitious, provides. As the King proclaims with an almost child-like – were it not for his immense power, and also responsibility – naiveté: 'No violence please. / Let ours be a regiment / of tolerance and love' (202). But the desire is doomed to be torpedoed by the gravity of ruthless power, where poetry simply will not fit. Such is the function of the character that Gaveston refers to as 'dead man Mortimer' (201): to smother joy; to impose orthodoxy; to eliminate the King in love, with the justification that this very desire for love, and for openness, is the cause of the kingdom's doom. Implicitly, the King is aware that such is the choice he is making when he aligns his desire to Gaveston and detaches himself from his wife, who, in turn, becomes closely aligned to Mortimer. 'The sexual impulses, too, are subject to control and repression by civilisation, which prevents happiness but, on the other hand, seems necessary for the maintenance of stability', observes Gritzner, after Freud (3). By choosing Eros, therefore, the King also chooses Thanatos.

Despite the variation in circumstances, the hypothesis also applies widely to *The Rest Will Be Familiar to You from Cinema*, where we are dealing, explicitly, with three marriages – Jocasta and Laios; Jocasta and Oedipus; Polynices and his bride [historically, her name, not mentioned in the text, is Argeia]. Even though the latter does not feature in Crimp's play, she is rendered present by means of a particularly vivid reference that Jocasta makes when she re-encounters her son, directly associating the current predicament of war-torn Thebes to his choices:

JOCASTA. But you've married.
　　And into a different world – why?
　　[...]
　　You had a duty to make me happy –
　　[...]
　　to allow me to fill the marriage-bath for you –
　　from your own city's sacred river
　　but you shut me out.
　　You shut out your own city.
　　[...]
　　while you struggled to locate
　　your child-bride's vagina.

(26)

The relationship between marriage and desire is not a straightforward one, although it is very clear that desire has been a key element to the constitution of each marriage foregrounded in the play. It is important to note that we are introduced to Jocasta through a monologue (albeit with interjections from the Girls), in which she recounts events that shaped both her private and public life, but, also, by extension, the lives of Theban citizens, since the early days of her marriage to Laios. The events concern Laios's visit to the Delphi oracle, seeking answers as to why no children are materializing from his union with Jocasta. Being advised by Apollo not to continue with their attempts to have a family, as he will be murdered by his own son and the rest of his family will encounter violent deaths, as we hear from Jocasta, Laios, nonetheless, persists:

JOCASTA. Laios comes home here to Thebes [...]
    and the moment he's through the door
        inserts his penis
    into my vagina. 'This one's for Apollo,'
        he says.
    It's my first orgasm.

                                        (10)

In the actions of Laios, already, we observe a defiance and disregard not only of the divine, but also of the civic; hubris at its uttermost. Desire over duty clearly also serves as a stimulant: Jocasta's account communicates her own dynamic desire. She then proceeds to share the story that leads to her marrying Oedipus – and to eventually realizing the bond to 'my own beautiful boy-husband' (12).

Desire does not evaporate; but it does give way to the magnitude of the tragedy. The four children of the couple, the sons locked in a deathly battle for Thebes (Eteocles and Polynices) and the two young girls, Antigone and Ismene, are the inheritors of the chaos, as are the citizens of Thebes, thrust into a war between two brothers who are unable to resolve their conflict for power over the city. '[A]ny attempt to redirect the focus of attention to the sphere of individual instinctual life may seem obsolete and ineffective, unpolitical even', writes Gritzner (3–4). But as she continues: 'Not so, however, if we acknowledge the labour of the *imagination* which is involved in our conceptualisations of and aesthetic responses to the drives and compulsions of the human body and psyche' (4; emphasis original). Gritzner's theoretical framework speaks directly to the concerns of this chapter when she additionally observes: 'especially in the aesthetic form of tragedy, the conflict between life/love and death is dramatized as an agon ('struggle', 'battle') between the mortal hero or heroine and the gods' (4). Gritzner is of course entirely right in that, in its traditional iteration, Greek tragedy is largely built on the perennial pursuit of the relationship between the human and divine; between authority and accountability. In Crimp's version of this tragedy, however, as we might also argue for *Cruel and Tender*, the gods are neither the ones to whom accountability is directed, nor the ones who will turn punishers. The accountability in Crimp's adaptations of Greek tragedy, on the contrary, is geared towards the people – the many, who will call on the privileged few to take responsibility for their actions at the face of precarity and mass suffering. Such is the case, briefly put, in *Cruel and Tender*, when the General's desire (the contemporary figure corresponding to the Sophoclean Herakles in *Trachiniae*) determines the fate of the citizens who are brought into a brutal war, or, also, in *The Rest Will Be Familiar to You from Cinema*. It is the individual preferences, choices, and, ultimately, desires of the few that lock the public into protracted and painful conflict with disastrous repercussions of displacement and death.

The narrative device that Crimp develops in *The Rest Will Be Familiar to You from Cinema*, where a Chorus of women (the Girls) confront the privileged minority (the royal family) that shaped the lives of the underrepresented majority, forcing them, in turn, to face up to their own choices, underlines the way in which this very accountability for desire is returned from the intangible heaven to the tangible earth. Crimp appears to be paying homage to the orthography of the source titles, and to their implications: the '-ae' suffix in both plays that serves as the starting point for *Cruel and Tender* and *The Rest Will Be Familiar to You from Cinema*, *Trachiniae* and *Phoenissae* respectively, denotes a mass noun that indicates female subjects of a certain place of origin. In both cases, and especially in *The Rest Will Be Familiar to You from Cinema*, these neglected, invisible subjects, are restored to their significance. It is subjects like these, in precarious positions, that become obliterated in the face of privileged desire and transgression, as we also see in the moment of confrontation between the impoverished locals and the royals in *Lessons in Love and Violence*.

Gritzner's syllogism captures a rather complex state: to separate the personal, the desirous, the erotic, from the political, is not a tenable hypothesis, even though it might appear that, in pursuing the former, one surrenders the latter. In Crimp's work examined here, the hypothesis is stretched to ask questions that are significant, despite the eventual failure of his characters' alternative routes. We are witnessing political reality versus utopia and the exploration of the presumed irreconcilables, against binarism – and without authorial judgement. What if, in pursuing private pleasure, one in fact dares to imagine a more complete, encompassing, democratic, way of being – and of leading? What if it is the power of desire, and of the boundless opening up that it generates, including to co-existence, and to a certain benevolence, that is conceptualized as a positive force, before it is smothered by the gravity of orthodoxy? What if, in that elastic space of possibility, desire becomes a form of transformation, of both self and other – of both self and state – towards a form of governance not bound to the restrictive laws of the past and towards a creative act of generosity directed to self and others? It is, perhaps, not unfathomable that the private transgression that led to political doom carries, at least at the point of inception, an almost naïve longing for overall happiness at its core; a radical assertion of self-will that can also be seen as a force of positive individualism, before history superscribes an opposing narrative. Such, we might argue, is not only the case with the King in *Lessons in Love and Violence*, but, also, with some members of the royal family we encounter in *The Rest Will Be Familiar to You from Cinema*; a quest for personal fulfilment that may, at least in the beginning, have been thought of as the foundation of a happier state.

On the occasion of the 2019-20 French revival of *The Rest Will Be Familiar to You from Cinema* (*Le reste vous le connaissez par le cinéma*) under the direction of Daniel Jeanneteau, one reviewer commented on the importance of Euripides's differentiation from Aeschylus by 'representing history through the eyes of a choir of women [...]', adding that 'It is this choir of women that interests [...both playwright and director]' ['L'originalité d'Euripide par rapport à Eschyle, c'est de faire représenter l'histoire sous les yeux d'un chœur de femmes [...]. C'est ce chœur de femmes qui a intéressé Martin Crimp, et Daniel Jeanneteau, qui met en scène la pièce'] (Darge 2019). Such a hypothesis is provable across Crimp's intertextual journeys: the point of writerly intervention in the historical narrative materializes through the probing of how the female element might be not only revealed, but, in fact, elevated. In Crimp's texts, *she* emerges as a sentient and engaged counterforce to the blind male political and military ambition, which has, Crimp's work suggests to us, all too often shaped history. It is at the stage of inscribing a possibility of interjection in the historical, but, also, in the artistic narrative, that Crimp undermines the heteronormative orthodoxies of state politics. That the female interjection may become foiled, that it might become weighed down by prevailing forces, does not diminish either its ferocity or its lucidity. Without discounting the class stratification that the pieces are also concerned with, or the different levels of privilege, and lack thereof, that they expose, it is significant that the role of the sage observer of history, both retrospectively and in real time, and of her who becomes an actor (in the sense of agency) is awarded to women across Crimp's radical adaptations and varying intertextualities. We notice this, also, to name an indicative example, in *Cruel and Tender*, where Crimp highlights the discrepancy between Amelia (the General's wife) and Laela (the woman with whom he has had an affair, the very motive for his military crimes) intersectionally, in matters relating to both race and class, without neglecting to show that both women share a dynamism and pragmatism, tempered with sentience, that the male military and political leadership repeatedly fail at.

We, likewise, notice this, in the behaviour of mother and daughter (Jocasta and Antigone) in *The Rest Will Be Familiar to You from Cinema*: an engagement with life and its major existential questions in the context of a civic commitment infinitely more layered and probing than that of the men – whether sons, brothers, fathers or husbands. Yet, there is a level of privileged naiveté that also emerges when Jocasta and Antigone face off with the Girls: to the latter there is no such option as indulgence; the need for survival interrupts the proliferation of philosophical enquiry. Meanwhile, in *Lessons in Love and Violence*, irrespective of our reading of Isabel, her agency is undeniable; it is she who drives the events that produce the King's downfall; Mortimer is a mere executor. Here, too, the angry folk – voiced by an anonymous woman, who offers a visceral account of the deprivation the people have had to endure – force the class issue: the articulate female subject comes in different forms. Yet, it is the astonishing final moments of the premiere production that linger, delivering the final verdict, while, at the same time, denying spectators its stage execution: it is the Young Girl, silent observer of the scheme of her own mother and Mortimer, and as her older brother is crowned King, that will take her revenge. As she turns a gun towards her mother and Mortimer, she prepares to deliver her own sense of justice, as daughters often do – as is also the case in *The Rest Will Be Familiar to You from Cinema* with Antigone, whom I go on to discuss.

In this context, it is the review that Jeanneteau's production received in *La Libération* that presents the greatest interest; here, the writer frames Jeanneteau's handling of Crimp's text as 'adapting Martin Crimp's play that proceeds from a tragedy by Euripides' ['Adaptant la pièce de Martin Crimp d'après une tragédie d'Euripide'] (Beauvallet 2020), going on to reflect on the innovation of the specific staging. To refer to the production as an adaptation in itself adds to the intertextual layers of the work. It also implicitly acknowledges Crimp as a canonical figure, whose own work, six years into the life journey of the specific play, can serve as ground for re-imagining. Referring to the Chorus, in Jeanneteau's production consisting of young, amateur (at that point) female actors, the reviewer describes them as 'incarnating the subversion and the hope' ['elles incarnent la subversion et l'espoir'] (Beauvallet 2020), a comment that helpfully underlines female agency in both the undermining of the dominant masculine narrative of history and in sowing the seed of potential change; of difference. It is significant that the role is not only entrusted to women, but, specifically, to the young generation – as Jocasta makes her exit, it is the Girls that will 'incarnate' not only the mind but also the body, indeed the spirit of socio-political sobriety, agency and justice. As the *Libération* critic also remarks, the young female actors are dressed in clothing – bright, contemporary – that reflects their age and spirit (Beauvallet 2020). The same is true of Antigone, who appears in the frame of the play's 'characters', rather than the superstructure that the Girls occupy in the play as omniscient observer-actors. She is the perennial child par excellence, herself forever oscillating, as her mother, between the private and public domains: a girl on her way to womanhood, a royal daughter with a heavy state axiom.

Unmarried Women, or Desire for Democracy

'[E]specially in the aesthetic form of tragedy, the conflict between life/ love and death is dramatised as an *agōn* ('struggle', 'battle') between the mortal hero or heroine and the gods', writes Gritzner (4). She adds that 'The transgression of boundaries is a key principle of tragedy, its primary motivating force, and recognisable in acts such as Oedipus (unknowingly) killing his father and marrying his mother, [or] Antigone's defiance of the laws of the polis [...]' (4). Having discussed the former, here I would like to concentrate on the latter. And even though there is a vast difference between them, not least in terms of stage time and overall presence in the respective works, it is worth introducing this section by noting that both in *The Rest Will Be Familiar to You from Cinema* and *Lessons in Love and Violence* the royal daughters, Antigone and the Young Girl – however fallen their fathers – emerge as forces in their own right. Their relationship to the future is an ambiguous one, their own survival – or at least their public role – uncertain, but their civic agency awakens. Their shared desire is to deliver justice, to avenge the men they loved, whom the state destroyed. It is a force at least as strong as these men's catastrophic desires, while, at the same time, striving for a fairer society. And so, at the end of the premiere production of *Lessons in Love and Violence*, the Young Girl, at one point seen wearing the King's crown, turns a gun towards his persecutors; and in *The Rest Will Be Familiar to You from Cinema*, Antigone, scrappy as she is privileged, afraid as she is daring, a girl as she is a woman, awakens to the desirous duty: to claim justice for those she loves, and to understand the very nature and limits of love – towards herself, towards others – even as its hope margin is closing, even as it is slipping away.

The Antigone sections in *The Rest Will Be Familiar to You from Cinema* are fascinating, not only because of what we saw on stage in the premiere production, but also because of what we did not see – but which exists in Crimp's text. I am also struck by the intense similarities, but also differences in two of the major productions that the play has so far received: Mitchell's and Jeanneteau's. The staging contexts of the two shows were also markedly different, raising questions of privilege, but also access and fluid social contexts to plot pivots and content frames in an interesting way. I first encountered the play in Hamburg as an itinerant production, belonging to, but not housed in, the emblematic Deutsches Schauspielhaus Hamburg, at the very centre of the affluent German city. Rather, travelling on a coach, spectators were taken to the periphery of the city, and to a studio space, where, removed from the 'safety' of the institutional structure, the transgressions of Crimp's characters played out all the more intensely, both in a spatial vacuum and not (see Angelaki 2014). Out there, was a city – the one on which, one might imagine, the actions of the privileged family in whose home we found ourselves (on the basis of Eales's set) had catastrophic consequences. We were, therefore, transported to the characters' world, at the same time as they were becoming exposed to 'ours' ('us' here being the community; the *dēmos*), a point dynamically reinforced by the intrusion of the Girls in the family structure, as well as in the structure of the play. In her confusion as to how to navigate her life, and which space to occupy, buzzing with possibility and suppressed by the burden of responsibility, Antigone appeared as a caged animal about to break free – but without entirely knowing, or prepared for, what freedom might mean, and what it might entail as consequence.

Jeanneteau's production was also an itinerant one, albeit in a different way. To begin with, the show opened at Festival d'Avignon. When the production arrived in Paris some months later, spectators had to make their way to the peripheral T2G – Théâtre de Gennevilliers on their own chosen transport means; for the return to the city, there was a shuttle bus option, indicating the separation of the suburb from its urban centre.[4] Here, too, we were decontextualized – but the privilege was dispensed with. Here, *The Rest Will Be Familiar to You from Cinema*, became, in itself, a 'lesson in love and violence': the set was a classroom; the history lessons were being given (the Girls here appeared as students), as they were being learned – and, importantly, they were being learned by their actors at the same time as they were being learned by the Chorus, the Girls, the questioning students – non-professional performers drawn from the *banlieue*. Here, Antigone, a princess not too different in her youthful outfit and appearance (in contrast to the stark black dress she wore in the Hamburg show), and yet entirely different in privilege from the Girls, was going to learn how she would transition from precocious daughter to indignant agent. The city was out there – but the productions had crafted a space of action where we, as well as the characters, were immersed in a suspended moment of potential and change. I argue that no other character in Crimp's play – where the 'family' cast is concerned – captured the duality, as well as the radical fluidity, between past and future, life and death, love and desolation, more than Antigone, blossoming and wilting at the same time.

The significance of Antigone to the play is also indicated by the climactic moment in which her eponymous segment ('Scene Fourteen – Antigone') lands, with only one scene remaining to the finale. In the published playtext of the play (2019), the scene runs from p. 73 to p. 83 (the ensuing scene, where we once more return to the Girls, as they bring the play to its closing, runs only from pp. 83-84). The importance of the 'Antigone' segment, therefore, is notable – it is her presence that marks the last moments of the play, a whirlwind on stage, before winding down to the momentous, yet anti-climactic finale, where the Girls pose a series of questions as to the state of the world, oscillating between past, present and future, or between fossilized and lived history. It is important, then, to also observe that, as the author's note informs the reader, immediately following this exchange

OEDIPUS. Won't you kiss me?
ANTIGONE. No. Sorry. I can't.
[...].

(76)

'In the original production Oedipus was kissed here by one of the Sphinx-girls and a cut was taken in the text' (76). As Crimp's note further reads, the cut extends to all but the final five lines of the scene, where Antigone herself does not feature, and where Oedipus can be seen in a brief exchange with the Girls (83).

The cut is a drastic one, and the impression that the text makes with the omission of a considerable part of Antigone's dialogue is markedly different from what might have been. Having seen the original production, where, in my view, Antigone's presence was highly significant as a stage event, as plot catalyst for events that might go on to transpire beyond the structure of the specific play, and in the broader universe of Antigone narratives that one may be reasonably familiar with, reading this note caused me to wonder how much more intensity Antigone's presence might have delivered in these last moments of the production. Might it, for example, have even rivalled the impact of Jocasta, in whose deathly absence Antigone would be installed as the new generation with which some hope rests, in its rebellion, in its lack of compromise – in its heightened desire to do right not only by the self but, also, by the community, while, at the same time, struggling, in a nascent civic state, to ascertain what the very concept of community could even mean? And while the query might be convoluted, and the question a hypothetical one, it does merit consideration, as the Antigone scene merits closer analysis; such a view is corroborated by the climactic significance that the scene was awarded in the Jeanneteau production, where it was played in its entirety.

Although, as it progresses, and especially in the part omitted in the Hamburg production, the Antigone scene captures the fierce defiance of a young woman unafraid to clash with both her actual father and the person representing the paternalistic state structure, the power keeper – Kreon – it is essential to note that it begins with a significant long monologue by Antigone. Given the range and scope of the segment, the following extensive quotation is merited. Here, Antigone begins by voicing an objection to a statement made at the ending of the previous scene, where she is called a 'girl', listed by an officer as merely another item on the order of business (72):

ANTIGONE. What girl?
>   Is he talking about me?
>   [...]
>   What're you staring at, softly-spoken Officer?
>   Is it my clothes? Do I smell?
>   Or is it my hair?
>   [...]
>   Be brave be brave be brave:
>   I'm being brave *what is the fucking use*
>   oh and what do you think of my hair –
>   *Mummy* –
>   when I do *this* with it?
>   *She grips her hair with two hands at first in a 'pose' but then with growing intensity as if she would tear it out* [...]

(73)

I have made partial reference to this passage elsewhere (Angelaki 2014), and, as the opening segment of Antigone's monologue prefigures the gendered, fierce defiance of equally gendered authority that will bring the play to its conclusion, it is essential to return to it here so as to set the tone. In the first lines, Antigone, reeling from her mother's suicide as she is also experiencing the growing pains of womanhood and citizenship, flags two concerns: she will not be the princess anymore; she will not be prim and proper, as, arguably, she had never desired to be – hence the reference, also, to the reversal of the male gaze and the undermining of the female stereotype of the well-behaved, well-groomed subject serving the projections of others.

But it is in the section that follows that Antigone's political speech begins to take shape even more potently as she claims for herself the right to dwell not on aspects of the domestic, of detached privilege, of the so-called female domain, but on the city and state:

> Thebes is a city
> located between two rivers.
> To what does it owe
> its outstanding economic importance?
> Is it (a) to investment in new technologies
> (b) to the cultivation of olives
> or (c) to copper and tin
> or (d) to copper and tin
> [...]
>
> (73)

Eventually, Antigone grows exasperated, shouting 'TICK ONE BOX ONLY!' (74) to all and no one in particular – the same feeling that her entire scene emanates: this is an anger at the state of affairs that Antigone is coming into; a world drained, destroyed. Her conscience is a civic one, and it is particularly noteworthy that, in this excerpt, Crimp infuses a significant environmental element. In so doing, he exposes human greed – the archetypal cause for hubris – which the text associates with military-capitalist transgression that has displayed callous disregard for landscape, mining the city to advance political agendas. The result is annihilation. Antigone, a creature of her city in a pure, unmediated, unmarred by ambition desire for her state's well-being, begins with an emphasis on landscape: the two rivers that make the city enviable, and desirable; the natural element that is eclipsed by hunger for power and dominance, the likes of which she is now, like the people of the city, experiencing the consequences of. Beyond all

else that adds to her extraordinary domestic and public crisis, Antigone
is also a young person, inheriting a wounded, depleted natural world in
whose destruction she has played no role, but in the aftermath of whose
apocalyptic imagery she must now forge an existence.

As the scene develops, Antigone not only enters, but, indeed, escalates direct confrontation with both Oedipus and Kreon, as indicated
above. She may have antithetical feelings towards each of them – a love
for her father; a disdain for Kreon – but she is on the same collision
course towards questioning, equally, any play for authority that either
man could make over Thebes. When Oedipus asks Antigone to state
her love for him, she refuses, without explanation or justification (74);
when he asks her to kiss him (as before, in reference to the script 'cut'),
she also refuses. And even though her defiance of her father's authority or jurisdiction over her is emphatic and dramatic – for example,
towards the end of the scene, when Oedipus invites her to pack so
they can leave in a hurry, she exposes his delusion, and his clinging
on to material remnants of a life that no longer exists by asking 'How
are we going to *live*?' (83) – it is in Antigone's interactions with Kreon
that her resistance lands with the most compelling force and maturity.
Kreon audaciously announces that as Antigone is to marry his son 'the
consequence is: authority rests with me' (77), a statement that unilat-
erally assumes simultaneous, automatic, unequivocal jurisdiction over
a woman's body and over a city. It is, in fact, Antigone's body that is
meant to procure this very rule through its function as an instrument of
the state. By marrying Kreon's son, Antigone will legitimize his rule,
returning, notionally, the city to some degree of stability towards the
next stage in its history.

But Antigone imagines for herself a different role as civic subject.
While Oedipus – ironic at first, then literal – effectively pleads with
Kreon to retain him in the governance structure of the state, which
Kreon refuses under the same breath as ordering the unceremonious
disposal of Polynices's body, it is Antigone who proclaims that this is
anti-constitutional, showing a combative stance that Oedipus attempts
to curb, to no avail; Antigone is determined (78-79). As Kreon's con-
descension towards her grows, Antigone raises her voice higher, repeatedly resisting being described as a child by Kreon (79) and now coming
fully into her own, defending her family as she defends the city. Not
only does she not retreat, but, in fact, intensifies her attack, advocating
both for her father's right to remain in Thebes and her brother's right
to a proper and respectful burial (79). We have heard Kreon refer to the
toxicity of Polynices's corpse (79). Antigone immediately confronts the

unfounded claim, as well as Kreon's authority in making such a pro-
nouncement (revealed to originate in the desire of Eteocles) (79). She
perseveres in her protest, as Kreon continues to use demeaning, gendered language towards her (80), in attempts to undermine her agency.
She will not be thwarted; rather than retreat, she persists in her questioning, reversing the roles that Kreon is attempting to establish and
striving for her own vision of state and city.

The so-called toxicity of Polynices's body is, we can reasonably
argue, meant by Kreon as both physical and conceptual: as an enemy,
Polynices is considered a *miasma*, and the ritual burial of his body will
also produce dire consequences for anyone undertaking it; meanwhile,
as a political and military figure Polynices is, likewise, associated
with doom and destruction and, therefore, has no place in Thebes.
Antigone, though, resists the notion that such a dismissal can rest in
the hands of one man only: with argument and reason she attempts to
reverse Kreon's reading of state and history, proving herself sober in her
argumentation despite the emotionally charged and physically drained
context (having returned from the battlefield, where her mother has
committed suicide) in which she finds herself.

It is important that, in this moment, Kreon seeks a prompt from
one of the Girls in retracing his version of history. That it eludes him
is not only an indication of the problematizing of time and conventional dramaturgy that Crimp undertakes here, but, also, of the play's
troubling of the plausibility of orthodoxy in the version of history – or
of the myth – that has become instituted as narrative unchallenged
and uncontested. In her dramaturgical function as intertextual and
cross-historical device, it is now Antigone's role to upset the narrative.
The following exchange is indicative:

GIRL. Polynices is an enemy / of the state.
KREON. Is an enemy of the state. Thank you.
ANTIGONE. What 'state'? this is his home.

(80)

Denied support by Oedipus, whose help she seeks, on the grounds of
the fact that, as he proclaims, she will be killed by Kreon if she persists, and, likewise, lacking aid from all others on the stage (the Girls;
the Officer), Antigone, fearless, moves to the body and '*kisses Polynices'
mouth*' (81). The section demonstrates Antigone's – and by extension
Crimp's – upsetting of the binary between private and public; as I have
also discussed extensively in earlier work (2012), Crimp's theatre shows

emphatically that binaries cannot be upheld. The relationship between individual and society is fluid and symbiotic, rather than fragmented and distinct. As Antigone protests, the city is her brother's home; this applies literally to the family estate, and also more broadly to the city as cradle of its citizens. It is this bond that for Antigone is irreversible, irrevocable. The city is family, it is home. The ecology is as dynamic and evolving, as it is firmly rooted and not erodible.

Antigone's desire is multifaceted: it concerns civic and familial justice as much as it concerns jurisdiction over her own body, for which she rightly deems herself the sole controlling party. In the French production spectators had the possibility of observing these traits articulated in considerably more detail than in Hamburg given the editing of the text, but it is important to note that both actors who held the role, Sophie Krauß (Hamburg) and Solène Arbel (Paris) brought to Antigone an equal intensity and tender ferocity, as needed for a character who is forever oscillating between childhood and womanhood, as well as between what is right for the state and for oneself, moved by the sheer instinctive conviction and political determination that these do not constitute irreconcilable qualities. As her conflict escalates, Antigone's fierce resistance grows, performed equally on the physical, emotional and verbal levels. After she has kissed her brother, Antigone is once more dismissed by Kreon, who attempts to neutralize her presence and diminish her political agency by banishing her to her room; she is also, at this point, physically restrained by the male Officer, who is acting on Kreon's orders (81).

It is not a surprise, perhaps, that as the opposite side's attempts to mute and supress her intensify, so do Antigone's efforts to not only reverse the subjugating behaviour, but, even more importantly, to counterattack. In what is a particularly powerful moment in the dramaturgy of the play, I propose that it is in what directly follows that the scene reaches its ultimate climax. Here, we might detect the Antigone that we recognize from previous texts; from the extant philology around her character, and the civic disobedience symbolism that has followed her name through the centuries. But Crimp's Antigone is more than a reiteration, and more than a supertext: with his depiction of Antigone, Crimp creates a flesh-and-blood character that not only holds her ground in the contested locus of womanhood in contemporary society – her rights; her access; her voice – but, also, adds to the myth of the heroine as it has been passed on through generations of readers, spectators and commentators, both proceeding from and being in dialogue with these and, at the same time, being entirely unique, avoiding clichés.

The way in which Crimp handles Antigone's attitude towards companionship, partnership and marriage is indicative of this textual intervention and innovation, and captured in the below-quoted extract, which immediately follows the incident with Kreon and the male Officer, as narrated above:

ANTIGONE. I don't have to marry.
    I don't have to give you 'authority'. Let me go.
KREON. Oh? What's the alternative, sweetheart?
    Providing sexual services to the military?
    [...]
ANTIGONE. I'll kill him.
    Then you'd have no sons at all.
    You'd know what it felt like you cunt.

(81)

Having witnessed Antigone's tenderness towards her dead brother, and, by extension, her family and her city – the latter two, to her, are indistinguishable – we are now, also, witnessing her cruelty. It is important, however, to note that nowhere do we see a dismissal of Antigone's feelings towards her would-be husband (though his name is not mentioned here, we know intertextually that this is Haemon, Kreon's son). What we see here, rather, is Antigone's steadfast and aggressive counteraction of Kreon's continuous gendered dismissals and casualization of her physical exploitation and political instrumentalization. Antigone recognizes the threat directed her way by Kreon, namely, that as a female she is reduced, insignificant, precarious, and can only have one kind of function in the city, were she to be unprotected by the law of the state, as dictated by himself. That function would be to struggle for survival on the basis of prostituting herself. Immediately identifying the threat but without being visibly daunted by it, Antigone reverses the threat by deploying the same weapon – her own body – that Kreon attempted to activate against her, so as to emphasize that she is both in control of it and fully aware of its powers. At the same time, she refuses that it may be commandeered as an instrument of the state, intended to serve the purposes of Kreon's regime in its arbitrary dictatorial methods. There is no dialectical element here – no attempt at compromise, no plea: Antigone only advances, and does not retreat. In the second quotation, above, the first statement is decisive, fact based. The second already anticipates the consequences. The third iterates that Antigone is indeed driven by desire – and that desire may be rich, deep, dual – but here it is primarily an avenging of her family's and her city's honour, as well as of balancing the grief for the love and loss that she has experienced.

Moreover, the particular insulting word that Antigone uses against Kreon is not accidental: if Kreon feels he may appropriate the female anatomy for the purposes of his rule and power, then, certainly, so can she. Fearless and uninhibited, Antigone not only asserts her rule over her own body, but, also, reclaims the vocabulary typically used by men to belittle and victimize women, in the same way as Kreon has concentrated her own existence and value to only one part of herself, and uses it to prove her readiness for action. As Antigone appears aware of when she makes the bombshell statement 'I don't have to marry / I don't have to give you "authority"', the body can also work against its own physical and emotional desire(s), if needed, to protect a desire even greater. It is in that moment that Antigone realizes resolutely that the desirous subject and object may in fact be one and the same: a love of self and other that are equal; a love of self and city that does not set the one against the other – and that this kind of desire, this radical altruism, this resistance to becoming a bride – even if she may have wanted to – so as to preserve justice, is the one that her own body will be wedded to more than any other. In this, there is no compromise; in this, there is only freedom.

That in 2013 (and onwards) we encounter an Antigone so multifaceted, one that both encompasses and amplifies the myth, including that in the Sophoclean – and dominant, certainly also in scholarship – version, is a sign of Crimp's intertextual prowess, as well as an indication that the narrative was a powerful one to begin with. As a historical, comparatively early reading of the Euripidean Antigone proposes, '[…] when one remembers the phenomenal place held by this poet […] — how Euripides' popularity had made him more the people's poet than was any other of the Greeks, […] an *Antigone* as he wrote would have superseded all others in the estimation of the artists' (Huddilston 1899: 201). In the intertextual margins ferocity and desire swell – this is true, and so it ought to be for a text that survives and charges through time, remaining urgent. As with the other texts examined in this book, it is important to note that Crimp's work is distinguished by its intertextual sensitivity, but, also, its decisiveness. If, as others have noted, 'Euripides expanded the erotic theme of Sophocles' *Antigone*' (Scodel 1982: 39), then Crimp pays heed to this, amplifying it – and Antigone – even further. The object of one's desire, one's love, one's *eros*, in Crimp, becomes oneself (and her potential), and one's city; to care for and protect, indeed defend, the one, is to do precisely the same for the other; no less real is the feeling, than if it had another human recipient.

In closing this section, I would also like to underline the interventionist significance of this adaptation, and this Antigone. We know that it is predominantly the Sophoclean Antigone that is revisited; the one that stands as paradigm. Still, as scholars have commented in the recent period, Euripides's play, and his version of the heroine, not only merit attention, but are highly resonant to our contemporary world. As Arlene W. Saxonhouse notes in her remarkably lucid and astute reading of *The Phoenician Women* in its entirety, which merits attention as it stands, and whose emphasis on Antigone serves as a primary benefit, it is worth revisiting the Euripidean text 'because in it Euripides offers us another Antigone who at first appears as a retiring young woman [...] By the end of the play, Antigone has left the protective walls of her young girl's chamber for the field [...], for her confrontation with Creon, and for her daring journey out of the city [...]' (473). Saxonhouse's article contextualizes the Sophoclean and Euripidean Antigones, mindful of their differences and without reducing either to a lesser significance; her reading, rather, liberates the multitudinous essence of the character. Saxonhouse not only perceives the nuances of the character in the Euripides version intuitively, but, also, there is a congruence between this analytical vision and the version of Antigone emerging in *The Rest Will Be Familiar to You from Cinema*. Antigone – especially in her Sophoclean version – may have been even 'erotically exciting in her strength of will' (475), but what Crimp's version, in itself intuitively proceeding from Euripides, shows us, is how this eros might be an internal process, an urge that grows and consumes and excites the sentient subject herself, rather than one externally observed. As such, it is more aggressive, unruly – even awkward. As Saxonhouse notes, 'there will be no covering, no hiding [...] Antigone now plunges— without shame [...]—into the middle of the city's events' (487). Even though, as Saxonhouse notes, it may have been the desire of power blatantly displayed by Eteocles that spurs on Antigone's political awakening (486), it is, ultimately, a greater feat that is accomplished: not only the counteracting of injustice, but, most importantly, the reclaiming of desire as that purest, most essential of feelings; as the rite of advocacy; of agency; of womanhood.

Closing Reflections

A crucial action occurs when the King's daughter puts on the crown in *Lessons in Love and Violence*; an otherwise silent role, her signification as emphasized in the Mitchell premiere is the perfect match for Crimp's persistent quest to imagine and situate the female at the heart of all developments, whichever vocabularies we may choose to attribute to them: private, public, personal, collective, social, political, judicial. Not one of these domains is conceivable without a female agent, the works examined in this chapter show – as does Crimp's work more broadly – and it is her who will assert her presence, who will re-formulate the narrative, who will determine how the story begins and how it might end. As the *Time Out* reviewer noted upon reflection on *Lessons in Love and Violence*, 'The story's ending twists itself into something that's both feminist and a bit disturbing, one which weighs up the transcendent power of love against the pervasive weight of violence, seen and unseen' (Saville 2018). Nothing is ever straightforward where desire for agency and desire for justice blend.

History is an important thread: of literature and theatre itself, and of course, also, of actual events. At the centre of each of these two works lie spousal relationships and related complications: there are two marriages that are profoundly problematic in each case – that of Jocasta and Oedipus in *The Rest Will Be Familiar to You from Cinema* and that of Isabel and the King in *Lessons in Love and Violence*. The scale is consider-able: in both cases these couples are the holders of power by royal enti-tlement – any personal disfunction has direct bearing on governance. Affairs of the state, then, are intricately woven with personal affairs. And even though any marriage carrying such weight might conceiva-bly evidence the stress of circumstance through tension in the couple, matters here are made more complex still through the tangled webs of personal relationships and political intrigue that shape both contexts. But Crimp is not a moralist: through the range of characters that appear in both pieces, as well as of course, through the complex dynamics of their relationships, Crimp taps into that most intimate fabric of what it is that interconnects all: the desire to belong, to own another person's body and soul, to be loved and wanted.

Such is desire: once more, all-consuming and entirely unavoidable; profoundly inescapable for the mortals, whose hubristic clinging to power might fool them into thinking that they exist in a separate sphere; that they occupy a space above the rest. That is, after all, the nature of privilege: desire comes with higher stakes; if one wishes to experience it to the fullest, they necessarily expose themselves to its consequences. Crimp registers, but he does not condemn; he allows his characters to be high-strung, and the texts are both razor-sharp and profoundly com-passionate. Even the epigraph that Crimp chooses for *Lessons in Love and Violence* takes this tone: from Samuel 20:4, it reads 'Then said Jonathan unto David, whatsoever thy soul desireth, I will do it even for thee' (191). There it is, once again, that purity in desire: in how one may feel it, and in how one, with tenderness towards that other, may choose to perform it. It is important to remember this, for it is in such nuances that the distinctiveness of Crimp's writing takes root, and where it holds. As *The Arts Desk* reviewer observed in relation to *Lessons in Love and Violence*, 'Benjamin's body politic is warm to the touch, stripped bare and left bruised and twitching by the end. There is no poker here because the authors have found a far more devastating, savage weapon: love itself' (Fearn 2018). As the King, astute and succinct, demands in *Lessons in Love and Violence*: 'Don't go out into the world and call love poison. / Love makes us human' (198). The rest, as experienced by Crimp's characters, their versions and retellings, is a battle to prove the hypothesis.

Notes

1. All references to the performance refer to my experience of the live show on 15 December 2013 as *Alles Weitere kennen Sie aus dem Kino*.
2. All references to the performance refer to my experience of the live show on 15 May 2018.
3. For a recent discussion of the play from a Classics-informed perspective, see also: Cole, E. (2020) *Postdramatic Tragedies*. Oxford: Oxford University Press.
4. All references to the performance refer to my experience of the live show on 1 February 2020.

Bibliography

Angelaki, V. (2012) *The Plays of Martin Crimp: Making Theatre Strange*. Basingstoke: Palgrave Macmillan.

Angelaki, V. (2014) '*Alles Weitere kennen Sie aus dem Kino*: Martin Crimp at the Cutting Edge of Representation', *Contemporary Theatre Review*, 24(3), pp. 315–330.

Beauvallet, È. (2020) 'Le chœur antique, une bande de filles'. Available at: https://www.liberation.fr/theatre/2020/02/03/le-choeur-antique-une-bande-de-filles_1777012/ (Accessed 21 Dec. 2021).

Benjamin, G. and Crimp, M. (2008) *Into the Little Hill*, in Into the Little Hill Opera Programme. Vienna: Wiener Festwochen, pp. 14–22.

Church, M. (2018) 'Lessons in Love and Violence, Royal Opera House, London, Review: A Rolls-Royce Production that Could Use a Few Tunes'. Available at: https://www.independent.co.uk/arts-entertainment/classical/reviews/lessons-in-love-and-violence-review-george-benjamin-royal-opera-house-katie-mitchell-martin-crimp-a8346736.html (Accessed 27 Dec. 2021)

Coghlan, A. (2018) 'Lessons in Love and Violence, Royal Opera Review - Savage Elegance Never Quite Glows Red-hot'. Available at: https://theartsdesk.com/opera/lessons-love-and-violence-royal-opera-review-savage-elegance-never-quite-glows-red-hot (Accessed 21 Dec. 2021).

Crimp, M. (2004) *Cruel and Tender*. London: Faber & Faber.

Crimp, M. (2013) *Written on Skin*. London: Faber Music.

Crimp, M. (2019c) *Lessons in Love and Violence*, in Crimp, M. *Writing for Nothing*. London: Faber & Faber, pp. 191–232.

Crimp, M. (2019d) *Men Asleep*, in Crimp, M. *The Hamburg Plays*. London: Faber & Faber, pp. 85–146.

Crimp, M. (2019g) *The Rest Will Be Familiar to You from Cinema*, in Crimp, M. *The Hamburg Plays*. London: Faber & Faber, pp. 1–84.

Crimp, M. (2019i) *When We Have Sufficiently Tortured Each Other: Twelve Variations on Samuel Richardson's Pamela*. London: Faber & Faber.

Darge, P. F. (2019) 'Festival d'Avignon: Oedipe face aux tragédies d'aujourd'hui'. Available at: https://www.lemonde.fr/culture/article/2019/07/19/festival-d-avignon-oedipe-face-aux-tragedies-d-aujourd-hui_5491057_3246.html (Accessed 21 Dec. 2021).

Fearn, S. (2018) 'Review: Lessons in Love and Violence, the Royal Opera House'. Available at: https://www.ayoungertheatre.com/review-lessons-in-love-and-violence-the-royal-opera-house/ (Accessed 21 Dec. 2021).

Gritzner, K. (ed.) (2010) 'Introduction', in *Eroticism and Death in Theatre and Performance*, University of Hertfordshire Press, Hertfordshire. Access provided by Mid Sweden University. Available at: ProQuest Ebook Central (Accessed: 21 Dec. 2021).

Hejny, M. (2019) '"Alles Weitere kennen Sie aus dem Kino" von Martin Crimp - die AZ-Kritik'. Available at: https://www.abendzeitung-muenchen.de/kultur/buehne/alles-weitere-kennen-sie-aus-dem-kino-von-martin-crimp-die-az-kritik-art-472874 (Accessed 21 Dec. 2021).

Huddilston, J. H. (1899) 'An Archaeological Study of the Antigone of Euripides', *American Journal of Archaeology*, 3(2/3), pp. 183–201.

Marlowe, C. (2017) *Edward II*. Dumfries and Galloway: Anodos Books.

Saville, A. (2018) '"Lessons in Love and Violence" Review'. Available at: https://www.timeout.com/london/music/lessons-in-love-and-violence-review (Accessed 20 March 2021).

Saxonhouse, A. W. (2005) 'Another Antigone: The Emergence of the Female Political Actor in Euripides' *Phoenician Women*', *Political Theory*, 33(4), pp. 472–494.

Scodel, R. (1982) 'P. Oxy. 3317: Euripides' Antigone', *Zeitschrift für Papyrologie und Epigraphik* 46, pp. 37–42.

Spatz, W. (2019) 'Alles Weitere kennen Sie aus dem Kino - Münchner Volkstheater: Alle Enden sind ein neuer Anfang, auch die schrecklichen'. Available at: https://nachtkritik.de/index.php?option=com_content&view=article&id=16961:alles-weitere-kennen-sie-aus-dem-kino-muenchner-volkstheater-mirja-biel-inszeniert-martin-crimps-euripides-ueberschreibung-als-zeitlose-geschichte-vom-selbstverschuldeten-schicksal&catid=115&Itemid=100190 (Accessed: 21 Dec. 2021).

Weeks, J. (2011) *The Languages of Sexuality*. London: Routledge.

Afterword

Forever Cruel and Tender

It is neither purposeful nor, in fact, possible to provide a conclusion to a narrative that is ongoing; any claims we make will be, to an extent, provisional, and subject to change. It was essential to recognize this at the time of my first monograph on the work of Martin Crimp, and it is as important to acknowledge it today – as I write these lines, almost ten years later. In these ten years, the world has changed in ways perhaps unfathomable, from the climate crisis and the COVID-19 pandemic to social media domination and the questioning of all possible narratives that we may have held to be true. Yet, narratives, as concept and practice, somehow, endure – especially literary narratives, which show a resilience remarkable, and which manage, against the odds or, perhaps, because of this very harsh and saturated socio-political environment that we find ourselves inhabiting in the early decades of the twenty-first century, to provide a touchstone for that which is the bare, unifying core of human existence. That existence, beyond binaries and boundaries, becomes a flow of thoughts and emotions; desire and devastation, pain and jubilation – the enhancement of the human condition. However many new triggers, methods and dialogues have been added to this process as we find new ways of communicating, and as the theatre tests its devices and is tested by conditions unprecedented, the core of the fact remains: words; bodies; longing; the touch; preservation. Such is the domain of the texts by Martin Crimp that this book has concentrated on. That words proliferate as they do, that they release a force of language almighty and yet so thoughtfully handled is a result of Crimp being Crimp: a master of speech; of the human condition; of the nuanced ways in which individuals attempt to connect to each other and to themselves; to want something and someone; to stake their non-negotiable territory, however threatened, however contested.

The way in which Crimp handles narratives of the past – literary, social, historical – and establishes dialogues between different forms of artistic 'texts' across time to arrive at representations of how we live our lives today, and what it is that remains essential and irreducible about these, renders him, in my view, a category all by himself. The power of these texts is such that, as we read them, words take flesh. In a fortuitous production, where we are dealing with performance texts, remarkable revelations on what it is that drives and sustains the human have the capacity to occur. Somewhere, in the space of all these years, in all this work, this impressive, diverse canon that Martin Crimp has built, two words persist: 'cruel'; 'tender'. They speak to the title of the 2004 play that, in my view, continues to be, also because of its extraordinary premiere production, which, intuitively directed by Luc Bondy and an international co-commission, captured the deepest essence of Crimp as a playwright, a touchstone, as far as Crimp's writing and its sensibilities are concerned. Cruelty is not merely about aggression and tenderness is not solely about kindness; their nuances are different – together they leave a trace on the skin, like Crimp's language does, that is visceral, and unnameable. No sufficient qualifiers exist, ultimately, for the full impact of Crimp's writing – I have called it, previously, a 'defamiliarization *affect*' (Angelaki 2012: 182). So it remains – but as the work progresses, and deepens even further, we need to be mindful that the experience of a text, and of a performance, precisely because it is so intuitive as to how we live our lives today, will always invite new terminologies. Interventionist intertextualities; desirous encounters; flows and floutings of all and every binary and boundary. The human experience is prolific; 'cruel and tender' is not a binary; it is both/and. As human subjects, we, too, are both/and.

In one of his – relatively – sparse interviews on the occasion of the revival of his play *The Treatment* at London's Almeida (2017), Martin Crimp spoke to *The Guardian*; the journalist, probing as to the content of the – at the time – forthcoming opera *Lessons in Love and Violence*, drew on the title, as Crimp was bound to protecting the content of the as yet unseen work, to comment that it seemed 'like a decent summary of his [Crimp's] back catalogue' (Dickson 2017). Crimp responded: '"I once wrote a play called *Cruel and Tender*" [...] "I hope to be both"' (Dickson 2017). In the laudation for a major Theatre Prize that Martin Crimp was awarded in 2021, the journalist and writer Till Briegleb closes his summation by thanking the playwright 'für all das Sanfte und Grausame', or, 'for all the cruel and tender' (2021). So it is. The gratitude rests, it strikes me, in being seen, recognized – not judged, not evaluated, but revealed, nonetheless. The subtlety, the delicacy between being cruel and tender, is such that it requires much unfolding, much exploration, many intertextual journeys – and, above all, the understanding that the space between the two is bilateral, elastic, a flow. The human truth is on both sides, or, more precisely still, in the 'together' space that both equally work to shape: in the mind, the body, the heart.

Bibliography

Angelaki, V. (2012) *The Plays of Martin Crimp: Making Theatre Strange*. Basingstoke: Palgrave Macmillan.

Briegleb, T. (2021) 'Laudatio: Satiriker des Schmertzes', *Theater Heute*, 5(May), pp. 34–38.

Crimp, M. (2004) *Cruel and Tender*. London: Faber & Faber.

Dickson, A. (2017) 'Interview – Martin Crimp: "I Wrote a Play Called Cruel and Tender – I Hope to Be Both"'. Available at: https://www.theguardian.com/stage/2017/mar/24/martin-crimp-theatre-the-treatment-almeida Page (Accessed: 12 Dec. 2021).

Index